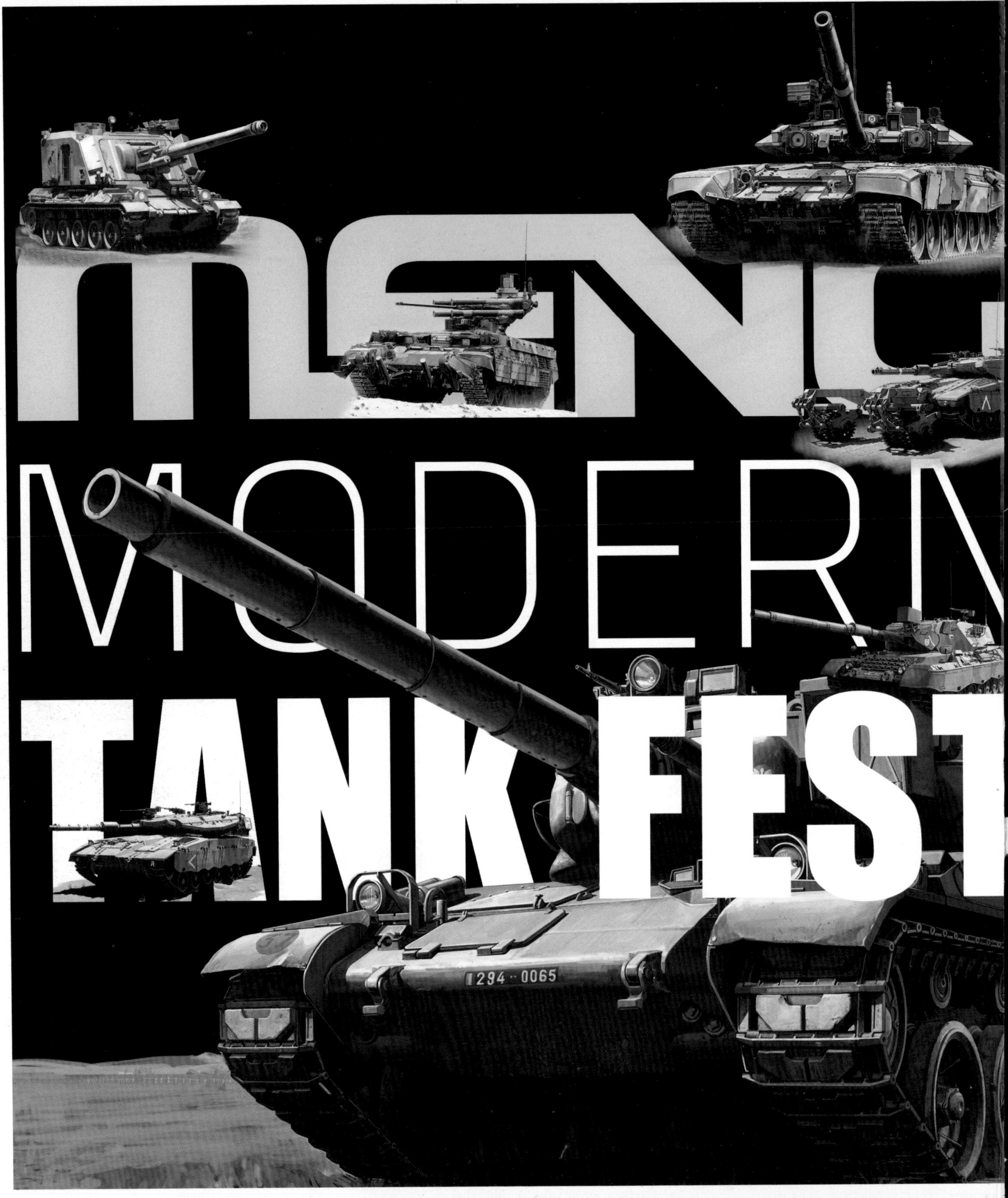
MODERN
TANK FEST
294 - 0065

TANK**ART**3

MODERN ARMOR

RINALDI STUDIO PRESS

contact information:
tankart@me.com

Graphic design, art direction and copy editing by Michael Rinaldi.

Author: Michael Rinaldi

Contributors: Andy Taylor

Published by:

Rinaldi Studio Press, LLC
105 NE Multnomah St. #502
Portland, OR 97232

www.rinaldistudiopress.com
tankart@me.com

Designed in the USA
Printed in the USA
1st Edition, May 2014

US ISBN: 978-0-9883363-3-9

Special thanks to **Rhodes Williams** and guest author **Andy Taylor**, and as always thanks to my fans, friends and family; without your never ending support, none of this would have been possible. This journey is just getting underway!

To all the dedicated fans of **Modern Armor** modeling, this book is for you.

3

FOREWORD

This is the Modern world.

Some time ago, modelers were limited by the available kits on the market. We only could build what few models were offered by the main brands such as Tamiya or Revell. Now years later, new companies have burst onto the market and started a new era of kit releases. It was once the realm of WWII subjects; we had new Tigers, dozens of Shermans, and even the rarest vehicles produced during that period, including theoretical tanks. At that same time, new techniques in painting and weathering were being developed to adjust those miniatures to look very realistic. One of the principal developers of that "revolution" in the painting was Michael Rinaldi. And thanks to him (along with a few others) many of us started to paint with another goal on mind.

Nowadays, we are a bit tired of Shermans and Panthers, and we look for new inspirations in the internet and the world around us. And what do we see? New pictures of the Wittman's Tiger in Villers-Bocage? No. What we can see in the media are images of modern MRAPS in Afghanistan, or great hi-quality videos of Russian Tanks in Middle East conflicts. And those tanks are as interesting as WWII tanks are. The times when people thought modern tanks were not weathered has gone away. We have seen Bradleys in the Gulf War chipped like Panzer I's, heavily rusted T-55s in Lebanon, winterized Leopards in Europe, or a muddied M-48A3 in Vietnam. And all these images motivate us to do new models.

Michael will show you with this third volume of his new **TANKART** book series that you can use the same exciting techniques to paint your modern subjects. Now is the time of the Abrams, T-72's and Merkavas. Don't be shy, take this book as reference and implement Mike's techniques to your own modern project. You will succeed!

And say "Hola" to the Modern world.

Pere Pla

This being the third installment of the revolutionary new **TANKART** book series I can now begin to expand upon my thoughts about the creation of this new product. There is always a tense moment or two when stepping into the business side of life and putting one's own name on the cover, it is an apprehensive experience regardless of the confidence level and the prudent planning. A few sleepless nights as well. I was never completely certain this venture would succeed, even though I've kept my faith in the fact that I really believed in the concept and what I was trying to achieve with this new line of modeling books. Could the efforts of explaining both the *how* and the *why* of the projects truly translate into a successful endeavor? Would you, the reader, grasp and embrace the books for what they were? And rolling into this volume based on Modern armor subjects, would it be received the same as it was for the German and Allied titles? Such is the stressful elements associated with this project.

As I mention in the beginning of **TA 1 & 2**, the creation of the **TANKART** series came about from my extensive library of models that really needed a new home that would allow me to open up and discuss the overwhelming depth of what goes into finishing models to a higher level. When I set out on this path, I had the foundation of the plethora of magazine articles to build upon, but the itch to layout a spread that had far less in the way of compromise normally associated with magazine work was such a draw. I had to do it. And thankfully, in the end when I started on the very first page of **TA 1** I felt the blood rushing through me and that excitement was palpable in the hopes I was creating the right product for the modeling market. It really felt like there was a missing element out there and these new books would fill that void.

I also put a lot thought into what type of product this should really be. I say that with the notion whereby everyday seems to push us more and more into the digital world, and what we know as analog products are not produced on the same scale as days gone by. Would a paper-based book be the right tool for the job, because believe me, I want these books to be viewed as valuable tools first and foremost. Details such as the final size, specifying the improved "Layflat Binding" to ensure the pages lay flat on the workbench, (to not close back on you), and also fit onto most bench top areas and still provide the space necessary to showcase large inspiring photos. Photos large enough where you can actually see the finer details to help connect the image to the context of the processes better.

In the end, I believed the feel and texture of a book sitting on the workbench was going to tie the work together with the reader's own work versus some of the other digital options available. The thought of quickly flipping to the right page and the ease with which it happens is very much a more enjoyable and engaging experience than sliding your finger across a tablet screen, as cool as it may seem to some. Modeling is an endeavor that demands your total concentration and focus and books work towards this goal in a superior way, or at least that is my belief. Does it mean there will not be digital format available for the **TANKART** series? No, but it is not a pressing issue and will be slotted into the working schedule when the timing is better suited on all levels to do it. For me it is not enough to simply click to the button to turn the PDFs into a tablet format, here too I would want the innovative elements to be integral to the design and I have the very real issue of utilizing a unique size for the book layout that will not immediately fit into the common tablets. So it is safe to say digital products are some ways away for now. As the company continues to grow, I will be able to allocate resources to those product lines in the near future.

Today, with the first two books in the marketplace, it is a different feeling that I have as I work on this volume. The apprehension associated with introducing a brand new product is replaced with a drive to push the books to higher levels, to divulge more information as I now have had many new dialogues with the customers and given feedback, which is helping to mold and shape my discussions moving forward. And that, in and of itself, is very exciting to be a part of! It helps immensely that the kit manufacturers have not let up and the constant stream of new releases, especially the steady flow of modern subjects has made the timing that much better. In fact, to give some further insight, we as the companies that make products are always discussing the popularity of the main subjects - German, Allied, and Modern. There is a very obvious reason I chose this breakdown for my books, and the one that continues to surprise me is the passion from the modelers of Modern armor subjects. It has really fueled the fire and I will actually introduce special edition titles in that arena in the coming months.

There was a recent conversation online in regards to the fact it seems there is more emphasis placed on finishes in today's model publishing and I would be remiss if I didn't agree with that sentiment. Right? After all, I am selling books specifically on that topic, so while I write this with a smile, I think the heart of that reason lies with the new kits we have today. It's a little like the automotive industry, where most new cars are excellent in there basic fundamentals, and so to with a lot of new kits, many are fantastic representations right out of the box and that naturally creates this situation whereby finishes takes on more importance to the general modeler. I'm in the corner that believes we really are experiencing a Golden

Era of modeling, and being a model builder today is such a fantastic reward for our love of historical machines.

It is with that level of enthusiasm that sees me sit at the desk and write these books. I don't honestly know how prevalent that feeling is in the hobby, but I certainly feel it. I'm very enthused and excited, and believe the hobby to be resilient and a vibrant growing industry. I know it is always fun to see what new models are clicked off our wish lists, but there is still so many available subjects yet to be kitted, and that means we are going to be enjoying this era for a long time to come. Your warm reception to the **TANKART** series has simply reinforced that notion and I, in return, will try to pass along all that I can to keep the momentum going.

MY MODELING PHILOSOPHY (revised)

In the first two books, my introductions spoke of the ideas I formulated from the previous years efforts as the basic concepts of my work. I've since had the chance to interact with readers in one-on-one situations and this has helped in my efforts to refine and adapt my own philosophy as well. I'm a firm believer in always being open to learning new ideas and the evolution of my own work is not something I shy away from. And from that, the evolution of **TANKART** will continue in a linear path and create a larger compilation of titles in my effort to introduce new material and ideas over time.

One such event stood out strongly when I took a trip to Toronto after the release of **TANKART 2 Allied Armor** at the request of a local hobby shop Hornet Hobbies that planned a 10th anniversary celebration and they wanted me to speak and give some hands-on workshops. This is a new journey for me on many levels, and I've not given a lot seminars to date (only two, in fact), so the opportunity to work with them was a great chance to be able to interact with the customers directly.

What was really special was it gave me a chance to expand upon my modeling philosophies in a personal environment and receive some immediate reaction and feedback to what I was saying and trying to teach. I learned some of my ideas do not follow traditional finishing practices and that "how I apply certain techniques" really needed more refined explanations to get the message across better. Things that will be specifically discussed in the following chapters in this volume. I'll make specific mention in each instance too, so you know where these elements are important to the end result. And getting that level of feedback was such a joy and inspiration as well.

From the beginning of **TA 1** to now, the heart of my philosophy lay in the concept that I'm not hear to preach the right and wrong of painting and weathering techniques, but rather to showcase the refinement of each process so you can make the best decision possible for your own projects. To me, this is a wholly new approach to the idea of what I am trying to present and the depth of this topic is now very clear to me as the foremost idea in the education of the myriad of methods and products we now have at our disposal.

My goal is to transcend to that level where I hopefully provide the depth of knowledge necessary, and by my own work, inspire and illustrate for you so you can apply them to your own models. My core principles of *layering* and *artistic scalism*, underscores the main goal of having the model presented *in-scale*, which provides the foundation for the chapter teachings. There is so much more than just the simple application of a technique, it is not a robotic endeavor and getting you (the modeler) to challenge yourself, to not fear making mistakes, to push yourself to new levels is all part of this for me. The beauty is you can take as little or as much away form these books as you need. There truly is no right or wrong, nor do I pretend to believe I have that level of answers, it's more along the lines that I have this skill set and ability to present these methods in such a way that I can help get you to achieve similar results.

The responsibilities for reality and artistic interpretation are now transferred over to you as a result of this shift in concept, and that lets you better utilize your research to create a superior model for yourself. We *must* be honest to this idea, while the draw to put our work online for sharing is in all of us, or most anyway, however the model must speak to you first and foremost. If you succeed there, the satisfaction in sharing and seeing the reaction out in the hobby world will be even stronger. It will come through and people always react well when we are honest within our own work. It is one of those very subtle layers of humanity that makes the creation of something special like a scale model very rewarding. What brings us into the hobby is often similar yet still distinct to each of us, and thus the translation of the subjects on the other end of the workbench are also similar yet distinct and unique to each of us. That relates to what I showcase in these books by giving you the tools of the trade to be able to express your ideas at the best level possible. It is not about speed, or the number you can get finished in a year, rather it is much more about being efficient with the work so you can be focused and rewarded with your own efforts and results.

Best,

Michael C. Rinaldi
February 2014, Portland, Oregon, USA

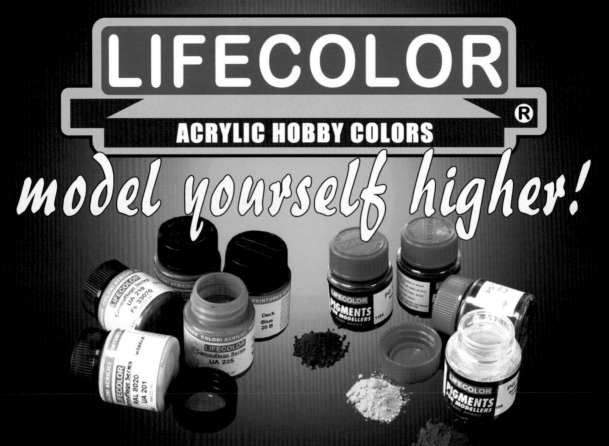

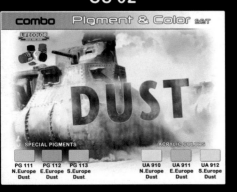

The chemicals. These are the products that allow us to do what we do, and at the end of the day it always helps, even if it's repetitive to a degree, to review what we have at the ready for the tasks at hand. The last 5 or so years have really seen an explosion in the various chemicals within the modeling market; new companies have arrived, and older established companies have introduced new products all in an effort to make our lives easier and give us better results. You and I both know this is a double-edge sword and the act of simply opening up the bottle in the hopes we will have instant painting and weathering success is pretty far from the truth. However, on the same note, most of these products do what they say they will do, (with some practice and effort on our part), and this is a good thing for us. In the end, whether standing in front of the paint rack in the local hobby shop or buying online, we have some great choices and many options to satisfy our various intentions. And that, my friends, is never a bad thing.

PRIMER

When push comes to shove, I have become more forceful in my recommendations for priming since I've started these books. While I tend not to be the one that preaches, in recent months with the first two volumes in circulation, and the conversations happening, I'm simply finding modelers having issues where they realistically shouldn't because they do not prime in the beginning. While we do have some choices in the product we can use, it really does help to lay down the right primer before painting starts. And as of this writing, the are a variety of newer choices in the primer market and I don't believe for a second these new products (from *AK Interactive* and *Vallejo* in particular) would not have been released without good reason. Seems I'm not alone in my efforts to promote the benefits of priming, with the primary reason being that we have added a layer of protection to the surface of the model allowing us to participate in more weathering efforts with less concern for causing damage.

Truth is, mistakes happen. To all of us, all of the time. I can recall at least one on every one of my projects. So mitigation is the name of the game with mistakes and proper priming goes a long way towards making certain the model is salvageable if something drastic does occur. That is definitely not a normal scenario, but it is prudent planning regardless. With that all said, stick with high-quality primers from *Gunze Sanyo*, *Tamiya*, *AK Interactive,* and *Vallejo*. These brands are well tested and proven to work in their respective processes and as I've said before, I've not had a paintjob go bad *because* I primed beforehand.

PAINT

The single biggest element in the finish is the paint, and what brand we use matters. For the purposes of the books and articles that I write, I'll talk almost exclusively about using acrylics. For various personal reasons, I have always been an acrylic user and my experience with enamels is very limited. Acrylics, though, are not a simple category of "buying a bottle or two, and off you go" proposition. Within their paint spectrum are a few major players and the type of acrylic differs, some are compatible with another brand, others are not. Like I advised in **TANKART** 1 and 2 already, I will stick with those that I am very familiar since I feel speaking about what I am intimate with is always the better path to take. Which basically means if I do not speak about a particular brand than that means I have not had much experience with them as yet.

New style colored acrylic primers are available now.

why we prime before we paint:

• priming a model prior to painting creates a number of advantages for us. First up is the adhesion qualities to the bare material of the model are improved upon. Typically paints are not designed to adhere straight to plastic, resin or metal and the addition of priming gives the surface more bite for the paint to hold onto. You'll get superior results by always making sure the model is free from dust and other surfaces contaminants prior to priming and painting. Wash the model with warm soapy water if necessary, make sure all mold release is off the surface.

• protection is the other key element to priming. Protection in the sense that the subsequent weathering will have a strong and ready base underneath because some of the techniques we use can be abusive to the paint's finish. While never a full-proof step, priming can keep the damage (when it occurs) in check and manageable for us to fix later on.

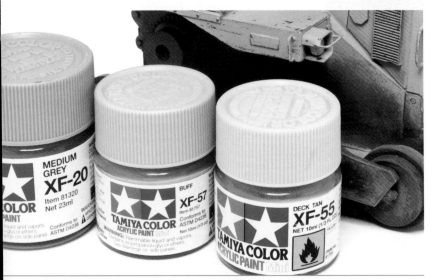

Tamiya Acrylics {Japan}

Lifecolor Acrylics {Italy}

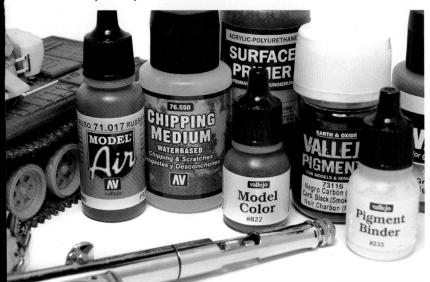

Vallejo Products {Spain}

Tamiya - for me, *Tamiya* acrylics have been a long time staple on my workbench. Access to their products was always readily available where I lived and that was the major reason I used them to a large degree, that and I worked a lot indoors so these acrylics took hold early on. And for those of you unfamiliar with them, they are what is properly called an *acrylic lacquer,* meaning (in simplistic terms) they share a lot of similar chemical characteristics to traditional lacquers. From a modeling perspective, this fact is important because it allows for them to be thinned with a variety of other chemicals such as Iso-based alcohol thinners, lacquer thinners, and water even. Personally, I stick with the brand's own thinners and water, but many modelers enjoy using various store bought non-hobby brand thinners. Either way, *Tamiya's* are very flexible, and I find them very forgiving and versatile for many of the techniques that I use today. Like all the brands I'll note here, once mastered they are durable and reliable products that give world class results, and that is what I am after with each brand I use. However, they can only be mixed with their own brand or *Gunze's* similar acrylic lacquers. Mixing them with the other acrylic brands is not recommended.

Lifecolor - where *Tamiya* is limited the most is in two key areas - color choices and the ability to brush paint. I have never succeeded in brush painting *Tamiya's* well, but Lifecolor is one brand that does both forms of painting superbly. They airbrush effectively thinned with water or it's own thinner, and they also brush paint exceptionally well giving them a very broad range of uses for just about every subject we have available to us. They are from Italy and one of the newer paint companies, and they have come a long ways in a very short while. Today, they sell a large portion of their product line in sets grouped together by a style or theme, such as IDF colors, or weathering paints for wood, and so on. They release new sets on a regular basis and nearly all of them have found their way into my production output in one form or another, their range of colors is broad to say the least. And as a nice bonus for those of us that paint exclusively indoors, they have almost no odor. Like *Vallejo* listed below, *LC* are what is known as *vinyl acrylic* and that essentially means they dry to a shell and this has unique characteristics that as long as you are aware of how this performs for certain techniques you can easily work within their range of properties to get the best results.

Vallejo - one of the more prominent brands today, *Vallejo* has a proven track record of providing us with outstanding paints. But not only that, as of this writing they have introduced a slew of new products such as colored primers, pigments and acrylic washes that are exceptional as well. In regards specifically to their paint line, we stick with the *Model Air* and *Model Color* series. The former is designed for airbrushing, and also has great brush painting properties too, and the later is really engineered for the figure painting world, and this translates to probably the best brush painting qualities available for the hobbyist. All the while, with the right thinning ratios *Model Color* can also be airbrushed as well. That being said, it shows that *Vallejo's* are an excellent all around line of paints and you will get a ton of use out of them. In the same vein as *LC*, they too are vinyl acrylics and they dry to a durable vinyl shell. And again, this means you need to understand this property to fully exploit these paints when using various techniques such as the HS chipping method. The other two key points with *Vallejo*, is that they are now readily available in any type of hobby shop or game workshop and they too have dizzying array of color choices. Combined with the new pigments and washes and primers, *Vallejo* is a great all-in-one choice.

How do all of these paints relate to a specific project? I tend to keep to one brand of paint throughout the course of the model's paintjob, so the decision on which to use, and when, usually comes down to the scheme I'm painting and what color choices I have at hand. It is not a popularity contest for me, they all will work great after some practice; they are a tool just like any other, and combined with a quality airbrush or paint brush all of them will fulfill our painting needs. The difference maker at the end of the day comes down to experience. (Get used to me saying this...I'm going to be repeating that a few more times throughout the course of these books.)

AIRBRUSH & COMPRESSOR

To achieve results along similar lines to the projects in this book series, the single most important tool is the airbrush and its associated compressor. In truth, to be able to hand paint a model without one to the level shown here is but for a few handful of skilled masters, and many of the techniques also require the atomization of paint to recreate certain special effects, so by and large having a good quality AB on hand is the only step forward if you are new to the hobby, and not just for armor modeling. For those of you on the experienced side and already so equipped, I'll try to add a few more helpful insights as well. For myself, and as of this book, I have replaced the airbrushes I used in the previous volumes with new ones. My old *Tamiya Super Fine* (.3mm tip) was replaced straight across with a brand new *SF* model -- with my old one I had worn away all the chrome lining on the inside of the cup and I felt it was time to retire that one. It had seen a lot of heavy use and always performed up to my expectations. Such is the world of *Tamiya* products...and the *MiG Productions* Airbrush is no longer available and I simply didn't want to continue working with discontinued equipment for the purposes of teaching. So I went back to *Iwata* (I've used them extensively over the years) and purchased a new *Iwata HP-C Plus* with the .35mm tip. Its quality is beyond reproach, you can feel it immediately when in hand. Such is the world of *Iwata*. But like the paints and other chemicals, I try to discuss only what I use, so if you have a AB from another popular brand and get great results, no worries, that is the key factor here.

Regarding the compressor, mine is still the fantastic tank-style *Iwata Power Jet* and the true advantage here is that the tank fills up with the pressure beforehand and this means steady, consistent pressure with only an occasional fillup as you use the air. This is a whole lot more efficient and lot quieter than your typical smaller compressor,

tips for achieving quality airbrush thinning ratios and air pressure settings:

• for a general paint-to-thinner formula, here is a good starting point:

• I begin by mixing a 50-50 thinner-to-paint ratio, and from there I add either more paint or thinner depending on my need for a basecoat (thicker), or a camo pattern (usually thinned more for tighter spraying).

• my compressor is typically set around 15-18psi for general basecoat painting. For tighter camo requirements, I will up the ratio of thinner-to-paint, and drop the psi to around 12-15psi and I move the airbrush closer to the model to achieve the tight patterns and keep overspray to a minimum. This is only a simple guide, but a very good one, and should get you going, especially if this topic is a source of frustration, or you are new to airbrushing. You will need to adjust for your climate and region, depending on humidity and temperature.

PRO-TIP: always, always, always spray in light thin coats and build up the color gradually. You do this to maintain the molded detail as crisply as possible. Heavy thick coats of paint will ruin the model's details. Also, the paint dries much faster and evenly, all desired properties.

My two double-action airbrushes: *Tamiya's Super-Fine (HG-SF)*, next to *Iwata's* superb *HP-C Plus* version.

Pinwash applied to enhance the molded on surface details.

which is constantly pumping while you spray. However, that being said there are new models in that range that are designed to be extremely quiet (compared to days gone by) and tolerable for close indoor work. The simple fact remains in either case, buy yourself a high-quality airbrush and compressor. Save your dollars and purchase the best one you can, search the internet forums for advice, and like a good car purchase, test drive an example prior to buying whenever possible. We all have different tastes and needs and there are great choices in airbrushes for all of us.

WASHES & FILTERS

The general category of washes and filters is probably the most misunderstood and wrongly applied products we have to use. Part of this comes from the fact, in traditional modeling practices of a few years ago, a wash meant a certain thing. But today we have narrowed the definitions and applications down to more specific processes, and truthfully it helps immeasurably to keep them clear and concise. I say this with the intent, if you are reading my books, that is why I get the results that I do. If you choose to pursue older application methods of these processes, your results *will* be different. I can't put too fine a point on this. If you cling to the notions of how things used to be done before reading my books, then you must be open to adapting to the style I am describing if your intention is to both understand what I am doing, and to apply these ideas to your own work.

In essence, I apply these two products very very specifically within certain parameters and what you read about from other modelers in today's magazine and book world is not the same as how I do it. Trust me on this point, and that includes many other well known authors out there. Speaking to my comments in the Introduction, this is one of the key areas where my conversations with the customers led directly to my assessment that what

I am describing in terms of washes and filters is more refined and extremely specific than what is the general interpretation of my work from the first two volumes.

To define them: A wash is a process of applying heavily thinned paint to create false shadows and enhance molded details on the model's surface so they stand out more to the viewer. I prefer to use the term pinwash to better describe the manner in which I apply my wash. What it is not (again in the context of my work), is either a single overall application brushed onto the model's surface as one layer (what I would call the traditional method), nor is applied over the details in a heavy, sloppy or quick manner. And I never do the sludge wash style and wipe back the excess after it has dried for a while, leaving the wash in the panel lines. Again, I say this to create a very clear distinction on my process, so you can better grasp the results I am achieving.

A filter is fundamentally a *tinting* layer. For traditional painters this is referred to as a *glaze coat* -- the intention of which is to alter the underlying color in a very subtle manner, adding visual depth to the affected area. A filter can be applied to a small section of paint to shift the panel's color, or as an overall layer to the entire model in a harmonizing effect. It is created in the same manner as a wash but only thinner, using 95-90% thinner to about 5-10% paint and can be applied by brush, or via an airbrush, which works great for covering the whole model. Where the confusion stems from is that the application process of a filter and the traditional overall wash are one in the same, and the results are extremely similar as well. Thus the reasons why having clearer definitions and explanations of these two important processes is helpful to everyone who reads these books. If I apply a pinwash and then a filter, I am not applying an overall wash to the model. This is a subtle yet extremely important distinction that needs to be made.

PIGMENTS

To provide for the most realistic form of earth effects we use pigments, now a *de facto* product and one that is in the catalog of a great many companies, including some brand new ones still growing in the market. Essentially, the concept of the pigments is universally the same across all the brands and successful application is generated by two main processes. The first being a dry application, followed by a carrier liquid to set them in place, and the other is a pre-mixed wet application inclusive of the carrier that is then applied to the surface of the model. The process can also be interchanged and used in concert as well.

More forgiving than paints, pigments perform very similar between the various brands out there. *MIG Productions* has been my long time staple, but there are now plenty of new pigments from *AK Interactive, Vallejo, Lifecolor, Humbrol,* **Wilder** *(new company formed by Master Modeler Adam Wilder)*, and a few more. But the trick to effective pigment applications happens when you premix multiple tones together to create more authentic and realistic effects. That's the real secret, it is much less about the brand, rather it is about using more than 2-3 colors to create your earth and dust tones within each range of color (I prefer Light, Medium and Dark mixtures). Once you do that, the results will be substantially more rewarding, and you will be able to control and recreate a much broader spectrum of special effects that you are after.

tips for achieving success with pigments:

• pigments work best over matte finishes, the extra grit within the paint helps tremendously with adhesion. Avoid applying pigments to glossy surfaces, it rarely looks good and is difficult to get the right look.

• pigments provide far superior results when you premix them into a range of color batches to apply from. Single color earth pigments tend to look overly simple. Instead, blend a range of pigments to create similar tones in *light, medium,* and *dark* mixtures for each project. Keep them stored in airtight containers, such as empty 35mm film canisters, or similar container. Mix the lighter colors first, then take half of that mix as the base for the medium batch, add darker tones, and then repeat that process for the darkest tone. This gives you a broad range of colors from 10-15 pigments in total.

• when applying pigments, I prefer a dry application then add the liquid fixer to set them in place. The resulting textures are extremely realistic *in-scale*. To do this, it works best to have your model propped up so the working surface is horizontal. Let gravity work in your favor and try not to move them after each application.

Pigments applied in various opacities to the D9R Dozer.

DEFINING WEATHERING

The creation of this book series stems from my desires to combine both the historical with the artistic into a scale model project, and because of the nature of armor models in particular, weathering is such a dominant part of this process. I consider weathering the state of the vehicles life at a particular point in time and how the effects of use and mother nature are combined together to make for an interesting subject at that specific moment. When it comes to modern armor subjects, we also have the elements associated with peacetime and this too can add an additional layer of information into the finish.

Recreating authentic finishes is only one element to the equation. **TANKART** means exactly that. There is an intangible element that comes from us, the modeler. We have to inject something beyond the obvious historical, or overly realistic effect, to create a piece that when viewed in its final form connects with the viewer -- tells a story. You, the author, must bring into the project some form of artistic elements to bring the model to the next level. The vehicle has to tell a story all on its own, sans base, groundwork and even figures. Those embellishments are there to enhance what the vehicle already brings to the table, so the weathering in and of itself becomes a critical piece of the overall equation. Achieve that and the rest will follow, and herein lies the heart and secret to the broader philosophy in play. When we look at modeler's work whom we admire, typically we will see a signature quality that we associate with that particular author. This concept is the artistic side of this essential equation and how it plays into what weathering is all about is the core for what **TANKART** was created.

EXECUTION

From there, the major hurdle to overcome is that most basic of processes -- execution. All the research and planning in the world is for naught if the execution phase, the actual implementation of the weathering itself, is not done correctly. And here is where I have to make a firm stand for a lot of modelers out there. The other overly common topic of conversation that I came across in recent months since the books have been released is the simple fact that way too modelers jump feet first into a project and use new ideas (to them) on their model without properly setting up a test session to achieve what I'm going to call *the most critical* element to success -- **practice!** Nothing gets around this idea, I cannot say it enough. *None* of what you read about in these books will come easily, *none* of it will look right the first time. *All* of these techniques, methods and processes require *time, patience, practice and experience* to arrive at a satisfactory conclusion. With that said, there are specific ideas I've developed that work towards this goal and will allow you to get to the next level in an effective manner.

LAYERING

Sitting down to extract the elements of my work created a naturally introverted experience, I had to come up with descriptions of my processes that made sense, were understood across all skill levels, and were easy enough to implement and repeat for consistent results. That sounds like a lot, but in truth it really helped me as a modeler too by giving me a deeper connection with my own work. I now had a clear concise understanding of what it was I was doing and how best to discuss it with the greater hobby as a whole. How this breaks down is rather simple in concept and thankfully straightforward to execute. The core principle that allows for all the techniques and products to interact successfully is the idea of *layers*.

The essence of the *layering* concept, which I have mentioned since my earliest articles, will always be dictated by the model, the subject's history and use -- the story *you* want to tell. Herein lies the bulk of the choices you will make as the author, so it helps to have an under-

breakdown of weathering principles:

• the goal of the breakdown of weathering principles is to illustrate how the seemingly complicated process of heavy and realistic weathering can be accomplished on a manageable level. Learning to create a balanced approach can yield successful results across the broader spectrum of your projects.

• define your projects goals, set a path that is achievable and that will allow for your success within your skill level.

• whenever you encounter a new idea or technique, set up a test session prior to attempting it on your project. Practice more than one time to better understand the elements in play to create the best chance for success.

• I believe in pushing ourselves to the next level, to seek improvement whenever possible. To that end, I will challenge you to absorb the information inside these pages and implement them into your own work for the purpose of achieving greater personal reward.

standing of each technique and how it's best applied to a specific stage of the project. And as with anything new to you, try to keep it simple and try not to over think the process. The basics will get you very far if you treat each step with care and work from less to more. Nothing defeats this idea faster than heavy handed applications, so know what it means to apply a proper pinwash, how to blend off the excess thinner, and so on. Each step, or process, will have it's own unique characteristics and this is where you must practice to learn the best approach for you.

I mention *efficiency* in the Introduction, and this was intentional because it plays into what layered weathering is all about. The concept stems from my own desire to become as efficient as possible within reason to extract the maximum levels of information from the subject as I can. In truth, when broken down and studied, layering requires less techniques and products and ultimately less time to achieve the same special effects desired. The by-product of this form of modeling is two-fold. One, it gives the project momentum to see it through, keeping the amount of "shelf-queens" to a minimum. And two, the enjoyment factor also goes up and this can't be discounted. We should enjoy this hobby, it is our time to relax, sit at the bench and likely with some good music and maybe a drink or two, really put down an effort that brings us personal rewards.

ARTISTIC SCALE-ISM

The overriding principle behind my work, what I pay homage to at every turn, with each step I am constantly reminding myself of this element - something I term *artistic scale-ism*. Having discussed this principle at length in Vol. 1 and 2, I will provide only a reaffirmation here to lend some additional insights into this idea and my thoughts on this topic.

"You can never have too small of a chip." This saying, one I'm very fond of, has a way of cutting through all of the clutter in regards to whether what we show on our models happens in real life or not. Often a very contentious topic on the forums, the discussion of "over-weathering" or "that does happen in real life" never really goes away. The epiphany came to me in the form of this thought is that it simply doesn't matter whether it does or not -- the guide should be whether it is *"in-scale or not"*. That is the difference maker and lends credence to the title of this series. I say that, bold and brash as that may come off, in the context that *we* are what determines what is placed on our models (even if dictated by reference photos), and that the interpretation be representative of an *in-scale* effect, which if successful in execution never becomes an issue in this regards. There is a very distinct and clear difference within this line of thought versus traditional modeling discussions in the past.

What happens from this line of thinking is very liberating in that it frees us from the overriding debate, which tends to become argumentative at every turn and this often squashes our momentum, our drive to get the project underway, and defeats the purpose of gaining enjoyment from the hobby. Principles of painting and weathering are not bound by the traditional rivet counting theories of modeling because each and every element is unique to each project, and when we thus take ownership of it, treat it with an attention to our skill set we can bypass this debate altogether. The results? Suddenly the work becomes enjoyable, the process, while challenging, is much more rewarding, and finally at the end of the day, we start to finish projects in a more timely manner -- all of which is geared towards the justification of our enthusiasm for this hobby.

using the graphic elements of this book:

• the design of the **TANKART** series is unique and all the elements were created for both educational and inspirational purposes. The book's concept was developed to provide the hobby with a more in-depth breakdown of the various nuances and methods used to create world-class finishes, in this case for armor models.

• the format was chosen to fit comfortably on your desk or wherever you might read the books. The long chapter lengths and page layouts are designed specifically to allow for the maximum amount of large, clear and inspiring photography, the physical manifestation of the models via imagery is the best way to communicate the results of each step so this was a top priority of the design.

• the binding is a special *"Layflat Glue Binding"* that is specifically designed to allow a softcover publication to open and lay flat via unique cover hinge and flexible resin glue that holds the internal pages separately from the spine as the book is opened.

• the text supports the photography in two very important ways. So important, the text was separated into two distinct sections for each chapter. Taking the premise of a traditional photo caption much further, the idea behind the text in the colored boxes is to provide you with as much insight into the mental and emotional reasons for each step of the process on each project. Basically a description of the *"why"* I am doing what I am doing. The regular text in the white space is much more traditional model building story telling about *"how"* the project came to be, its unique aspects of the kit and subject, and the step-by-step (SBS) process from start to finish. Combined together these textual elements also provide maximum information within each chapter with the goal to leave no stone unturned.

• the other graphical element that is a twist on a traditional call-out method are the thin white circles that adorn a number of the images in each chapter. Often when a caption is attached to a photo it is not always clear what is being discussed, so these circles help in that regards to connect the text to the photo is a very precise manner.

COMBINING HS & OIL PAINT

In-depth discussion of these powerful techniques used in concert

HS & OPR TECHNIQUES

In recent years, the establishment of these two important techniques has fundamentally changed my painting and weathering efforts, and the way I approach a subject's paintjob. I wrote at great length about each process within **TANKART 1 & 2**, and here in **TA 3** I will explore the way in which they work in concert together to achieve the end results that I'm after.

When I prepare a new model, I like to think about the HS technique as a *painting* process. Typical use of HS tends to occur immediately when I start to paint as the basis for nearly all the chipping and scratches I want to illustrate. I say this because if I know where I am going with the finish before I begin, I can plan the processes better and this will result in a superior finish, plus the path is much simpler to navigate. We get to that point with good photo reference, and then I try to add something special to the project that will further help guide me along, for example I want to try a new idea on this finish. This keeps my work fresh, exciting and avoids too much repetition between projects.

In regard to using the HS technique, I can set about deciding my colors and the order in which I want to spray and chip them. Naturally, each project will be different and I look at the model and discern the general chipping, say if the model is a winter or a desert piece. All said, these are the parameters that will set the tone for the painting. When I move onto the weathering, the OPR technique will fall in line with the path laid forth with the painting. All of those marks I applied are now the guidelines for me to pursue the patina that I want to represent within the finish. The point being I can create a model's paintjob with these two primary techniques, which greatly simplifies my efforts and makes the entire process a lot more efficient and ultimately enjoyable, and less stressful.

HS CHIPPING EFFICIENCY

The point of this effort is to promote the inherent efficiency that comes from this thought process. The goal of this discussion is to illustrate how it can fundamentally readjust your basic steps and allow for greater gains in both mastering these techniques and the end results will be improvements over time in your own work. The one caveat that needs to be mentioned again is that you will not be perfect with these ideas out of the gate -- it will take time, practice and ultimately experience to truly get the best results from each one. Understand and embrace this, and good things are going to happen.

The other reason that can't be overlooked is simply how realistic the end results can be. This plays perfectly into my adage of *artistic scale-ism* and gives us the right tool for the tasks at hand. Once you are comfortable with the techniques, you can see how you can adjust, maneuver and gain control as the author and truly be successful with your projects. It is a very powerful train of thought that also brings a lot of rewards and enjoyment to each project.

EXECUTION OF HS

While I have written two chapters dedicated to the HS technique so far in the previous two volumes, it is still very prudent for me to elaborate on the process and provide both a review of the steps, and allow for new readers to be on the same page as well.

It starts with the right product, and for those that have difficulty with HS product choices, I will write a short bit on using the newer chipping fluids for this technique too. In truth, the process is essentially the same and it's not a big change other than the use of the airbrush as the applicator vs. the aerosol can. The main reason I stick with the HS process is because of this, and my preference is simply for a quick reach of the can of HS to spray my particular subject and not be overly involved with AB prepping and cleaning. But again, the actual concept and execution of either HS or chipping fluid is the same.

The correct amount of water being applied, the smaller brush allows for greater control.

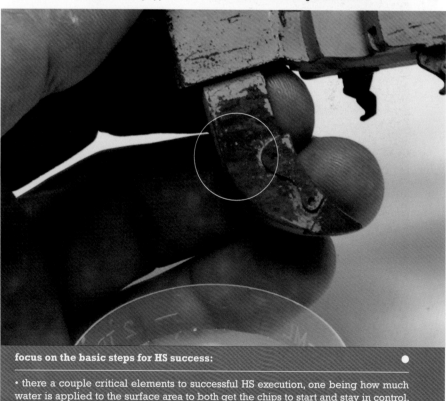

focus on the basic steps for HS success:

• there a couple critical elements to successful HS execution, one being how much water is applied to the surface area to both get the chips to start and stay in control. I have always promoted the principle of working in small sections to maintain the right amount of water on the surface and how much you can chip at one time. These photos show a typical amount of water that I use when I work the area in this regards.

working with the motion of the brush to create the best type of wear and tear in the paint: ●

• the motion of the brush is crucial to create certain styles for the chips and scratches. Use a motion related to the type of action that was likely to create the wear in the top layer of paint. Use the various elements of the brush itself to affect the marks, such as standard scrubbing brush stroke, or lean the brush back and use the sides of the bristles to skip across the surface, or stipple and flick with the end of the bristles to create a wide variety of chips and scratches. Keep your hand in control and work in the direction the marks would most likely occur.

thoughts on how successful the results are from these newer chipping techniques: ●

• the sheer power and ability of the various chipping processes today is clearly evident in this photo. While I tend to stick with the HS for most of my chipping processes, the newer chipping fluids on the market will work in exactly the same manner. I do not alter my methods for either product; it's really about convenience and having to use the airbrush to apply the chipping fluid vs. the aerosol can. We are very fortunate in this day to have these options available, the amount of control we can achieve *in-scale* is unrivalled in the hobby. I find the results so convincing that the satisfaction gained has really helped me mentally remain focused and reduce the stress levels associated with sort of extreme painting effort.

• with any technique, especially one that is new to you, practice and repetition will be your best friend. Do NOT expect perfection out of the gate, you must repeat the technique multiple times to ensure you understand the process and can replicate it with controlled results to achieve success.

1) CRACKED PAINT: typically this means you have applied too much HS *and/or* too wet of paint too fast *and/or* you sprayed too close to the model building up the paint too fast. It *may* also mean the HS was not completely dry before painting as well. It could be a combination or all these issues at once.

SOLUTION: hold the HS can farther away, move it smartly across the surface, do not stop and start the HS on the model (remember two even coats, dried in between, and dry to the touch before painting). Hold the AB farther away *and/or* lower your compressor pressure, *and/or* lay the paint down in thinner coats that dry much faster.

2) CHIPPING TOO DIFFICULT: typically when you cannot chip the paint this is the opposite of the above issue. You may not have applied enough HS, *and/or* the top coat of paint might be too opaque. However, it is usually too little HS.

SOLUTION: if you choose not to keep that top paint layer, then either strip it off, start over and reapply the HS. If this is too much effort, then don't panic, continue as much as possible, then switch to the sponge technique and add more chips of the base color. Or if you are confident, re-spray some of the base color on top, then re-apply HS and top coat and continue as before.

3) CHIPS FLAKING OFF IN LARGE CHUNKS: typically this is the result of too much HS applied. The paint dried well, but once the water activates the HS, the ratio is off and large chunks of paint come off.

SOLUTION: this one is easier to deal with than #2 above, simply remove as much of the top coat as possible, clean the surface and repeat the HS and paint steps again. The same spraying tips apply, hold the model at arms length, spray the HS in a quick linear manner to lay down even coverage. Dry each coat in between and repeat for two even layers of HS.

---

thoughts on using chipping fluids:

• working with the chipping fluids, like the one here from *AK Interactive*, is no different than with using HS. It is still important to apply two even coats of the chipping fluid and apply your thinned paint appropriately. I use all the same tools to create the marks.

APPLICATION & CHIPPING PROCESS

The basics of the technique have been honed over these past few years and while I can explain it as clearly as possible, it is very important to consider your own skill set and how practice is necessary for you to gain experience and success results from it. It is absolutely paramount that you test this method prior to applying to your project, the risks of failure the first few times are high, so please take this advice to heart.

That said, when I apply the HS to the model I have a few key points to emphasis. Start by holding the model at arm's length and spray the HS with a quick motion along the length of the model. Prudent aerosol technique is to start spraying before you hit the model, and stop it after you move past the rear end. Do not stop and start the HS on the model itself, this will lay down far too much at once. I use quick linear motions, and do not linger over the surface. Dry each layer in between, and for most effects two even layers of HS is appropriate.

Dry the model off completely, I make use of a hair dryer on low heat to speed it up and ensure the HS is totally dry. It should be dry to the touch and have a semi gloss sheen to the surface. Once ready, you can spray the paint immediately afterwards. For heavier chipping effects thin the paint with water (such as a white wash), and for the effects requiring less chipping acrylic thinners are fine to use. But the fundamentals of airbrushing still apply, ensure your thinning ration and air pressures are suitable to the task.

thoughts on developing a new weathering concept: ●

The text on the following pages is an introduction to a new concept in weathering that I have been developing over the course of my last few projects. It is early in its development and I will continue to expand upon it as I go along. Basically, I am using *oil paints* as the primary media for the majority of the model's weathering, which is a fundamental shift in my processes. The full power of **Oil Paint Rendering** is essentially realized when used in conjunction with the **Hairspray** chipping technique, and the resulting *road map of surface effects* is laid out for us to follow along.

WORKING WITH OPR TO MAXIMIZE HS

This is the first time that I'm explaining what I feel is the true power of these two techniques and how I am starting to use them in conjunction to realize my finishes. Over the course of the past few years worth of projects, my personal thoughts on my processes are continually evolving and the more I use HS and OPR, in particular, the more I began to realize the potential for the ultimate in paint weathering was coming to fruition. There were a few key areas of this discussion that would resonate in the larger scheme of what we have come to term as a regular weathering pattern of processes, however with OPR I soon came to the conclusion I could actually circumvent some of these more traditional methods to arrive at a new series of steps to weather my paintjobs.

What I am mean by this is we are currently used to certain step-by-step (SBS) methods that tend to fall in line with one another, and if we are not careful, this can easily lead to a substantial level of repetition within our own work. Two steps that stood out to me were the filter and wash steps. In simplistic terms, I was using them less and less and substituting these steps with more and more work with the oils later on to achieve essentially the same effects. The difference was that I wasn't applying filters and washes to the model as a whole and instead working smaller sections of the model in a controlled fashion that eliminated to need for these two as separate steps.

With oil paints and how I address the model with them in my OPR style, I could essentially achieve all the paint weathering I wanted with just the oils alone (for clarification, this conversation is outside the use of pigments for earth effects). The realization of this was a true epiphany and led me to truly embrace this concept within my own work to a much more substantial level. My early efforts with the OPR technique were designed to simply add the various weathering details in a more refined manner, but the more I used OPR, the more it grew on me that it had nearly unlimited potential to be extremely expressive for ALL of the paint's details and weathering.

There were a couple of very important results that came about from this new train of thought. One, I removed the repetitive element of taking a single color for the filter and wash to affect the entire model. If we start to examine our greater body of work, we can see how this is leading us down a path that will produce finishes to a very similar level. Same with the pinwash, and I can see it within my own work that rely heavily on these processes. But the power of the oils to work over a broader range of opacity levels, I can use them as replacements for the same effects filters created, plus the necessary effects I achieved with the pinwash. This was a fundamental shift in my use of OPR and my general approach to my weathering. It's more coincidental that it was more prevalent on my modern armor subjects because there has been a market shift to produce more of these subjects, thus it fits better to explain this concept within this volume.

So how does this train of thought and implementation of OPR relate to my use of HS and maximizing it's potential? It's rather simple really, and when you think about it, makes perfect sense. When you complete the chipping process what is presented is basically a *road map* for us to use for all of the weathering that follows. By accepting the HS results as our guide, we then work with the OPR to maximize each section of the model and its various marks and surface effects, and follow along with the efforts we have already achieved.

oil paint preparation: ●

• using oil paints in the manner we do for the hobby requires that we go through a brief but important setup procedure to ensure we get maximum success from their application.

• quality oils is important and we have a few great choices to use. *Winsor Newton* is the premier brand in art stores and *502 Abt.* and *AK Interactive* are the two best from the hobby industry. I use a mixture of these top brands for my models, and because the tubes will last many years the value is inherent even at the higher price points.

• apply small amounts of each color required onto a small piece of cardboard to help remove the linseed oil in the paint. This allows them to dry matte, and also blend much easier. Wait at least 15-30 minute before using them on the model, this will ensure the majority of the linseed oil is absorbed out of the paint.

• for OPR use, the less thinner you use to blend the better. It is best to keep your blending brushes clean and nearly dry, only the feint hint of thinner is required.

Here is the beginning of using OPR on top of the HS chipping to expand on each area, the depth of colors and the final realization of the surface effect. This is only possible when the oils are properly prepped with the cardboard palette prior to using them on the model.

The Caernarvon fender area was a case of less is more because it followed along with the notion of how a test prototype would look in a desert setting. But here the oils are perfect because they can be used in very limited amounts and still create a convincing finish.

The T-62M1 illustrates how oils can be used to enhance the tones and colors of the base paint and chipped areas, and be used to add subtle dust effects all within the same palette for the model. This attribute adds flexibility and efficiency to the weathering processes.

Thinking along these lines I realized that the hard part was essentially done for me. The myriad of marks that I created with the HS chipping steps were now the *road map* of the path I needed to follow to weather the paintjob effectively. What results is a reduction in the pressure on us, as the modeler, to continually try to manage and force these weathering effects onto the model, instead I felt much more relaxed and enjoyed everything a lot more. Basically I was using the OPR principles onto of the effects I had already created and the results I was arriving at were solely unique to the model in front of me, versus the more traditional approaches we have taken to date.

With a filter we apply the heavily thinned paint as a blanket to the model in an effort to tint and harmonize the paintjob. With OPR for this step, I am decentralizing the concept of the filter into smaller sections and what happens is that I am still tinting and harmonizing the paint underneath, but in a more controlled, refined and specific way. By taking in the adage of working in small sections at a time, this changes the entire process and the resulting finish is wholly more unique from model to model because of this.

With a wash, or a pinwash in my case (since that is the primary method I use a wash), the goal is to create a visual acuity that pops out all of the molded on details and panel lines by increasing the shadows (and by default the highlights) of the model's details. We achieve this by drawing thinned paint in and around each detail, and when approached with OPR I do the same basic process, but the difference is I control each section on its own and I can change the intensity and even the color at will. Typically, we add one pinwash color on the model, and then layer up some darker ones to pick out certain areas like hatches and so on, and I don't change that thought process, I simply get more creative and fluid with the outcome of it via the OPR process instead.

I hate to quote a cliché, even one as cool from the true master Bruce Lee, but where I was headed with all of this effort was to truly "be like water" with my weathering and let the surface details and painting effects dictate to me the ebb and flow of how and where I apply the vast variety of weathering elements. The oils are so utterly competent within this realm that I quickly came to this realization over the course of a few projects, and began to fully embrace them for these tasks, including those two major steps mentioned above. As funny as it sounds, I found that it worked. The concept of controlling all the weathering (up to the use of pigments) with only the oils was a true success and one I could adapt to any project. The was a bit of milestone for me.

And I hope by expressing these thoughts in this discussion I can bring forth another level of weathering possibilities to the hobby as a whole. What's happening now from this thought is that each new model is becoming more unique with the variances of the weathering between the models as I produce more and more, and probably most important of all is that the creative freedom of utilizing a more flexible process is breaking me out of some of the more monotonous tasks I undertake with the weathering. Overall, both the model and myself (as the author) are becoming more efficient as a cohesive unit, and I'm more relaxed and enthusiastic at the same time, there is less stress in general. The constant release of new kits shows no signs of easing up, and this new train of thought and execution of finishes is a great option to use on each new project. That is not to say the more traditional processes cannot still be used, but in essence I am discussing a new option to arrive at the end results for each model's goals.

EXECUTING OPR

When I discussed OPR in the first two **TANK**ART volumes, I gave a thorough explanation of the idea and the application process, and here I will expand upon those topics and go deeper into the actual implementation of the oil painting to further your knowledge of how best to achieve successful results. Like any technique, there is an envelope of use that we can derive from it, and thankfully oils have a rather large set of boundaries to work within, plus they are most forgiving in the greater scheme of products we use.

By now, I am going to assume you are familiar with the outline of applying the oils to a cardboard palette in preparation for their use on the model. When referring to the model's painted surface, I use matte paints and rarely put a varnish on, so you will not see me discuss "I sprayed a layer of Future" or anything of the sort. In fact, you want some grit to the paint, which helps in the defusing and blending of the oils. The brushes are also very important, as is the type of thinner employed with OPR.

For the brushes, I utilize a #2 Round brush for both applying the oils, and for some blending tasks. A good quality #2 Round is perfect because the bristles are longer than

tips for achieving success with OPR: ●

• OK, so how does this all work in the real world, or on the bench as it were? Fundamentally, each model will be unique, so let me discuss some general situations to use OPR, and then you can modify, or combine, them to create what you need.

RUST: use the tones relevant to this common element, work the rust tones in both a diffused manner to show "bleeding", and then the popular streak. However, I strongly recommend less is more with streaking, unless you have good photo reference for your project showing this effect is widespread.

FILTERING: just like the normal filter, you are tinting the underlying colors. This one is dictated by the tones of the model itself, but essentially use shades of oils that are very similar to the base, such as a light green oil on a green camo area to enrich the tones and add depth.

WASH: and like the filters, using OPR in lieu of a thinned wash is very easy and effective. I prefer to directly draw the oil into the panel line or around the detail and then blend it in and sometimes diffuse it out and away for more unique effects.

ENHANCING MARKS: here you are working with the chips and scratches to enhance the mark itself to look more pronounced or dimensional. You can detail the mark to go down to the metal, add rust and so on.

Step One - working on the side storage panel, I apply a thin coat of thinner to prep the surface. This will evaporate but what it does is allow for a smoother level of blending. Don't get it too wet!

Step Two - I start to apply a rust tone along the outer edges of the panel. I am using photo reference as a guide. Note the incredibly small amount of oil used and the precision of the application.

Step Three - I switch to a lighter rust color and apply this alongside the darker rust tone applied early, which will give a broader spectrum of tones and better visual results.

Step Four - Switching to a fan brush for blending, I carefully stipple the two color together gently pulling them to the center of the panel (up in this photo, but down along the top edge).

Step Five - within the center I apply a much wetter and thinned light tone to fade the panel a bit more. This will act like a filter and separate the part from the model in a very subtle manner.

Step Six - I then blend this color until it almost disappears. I use a small fan brush and stipple the oil I just applied in Stage 5, and the brush is nearly 99% dry, there is no need to use more thinner here.

Step Seven - the beauty of oil paints is that they are so flexible in their application. I often switch between applying them neat and with nearly no thinner for maximum precision and soft blending, to adding thinner to the brush and applying them in a wetter application, as seen here. I use the lighter rust color applied wet and this will eventually dry as a dusty rust tone on the exposed metal part.

Step Eight - I will continue to work an area and add more colors as I need to. Using this simple rusted spare track the tones are easy to illustrate for the SBS purpose, and basically I am adding dark rust tones along the edges and because the surface is already wet from the previous step I get a slightly softer transition in the tones for this small area. Again, a lot of this comes from the amount of experience I have with oils, and you will not get it the first few times you try this idea, but with patience and a LOT of practice the results will come and they will be as intended and the work will be elevated.

#1, hold more product and retain its sharp tip for a greater length of time. I find it the best all around compromise for the majority of the tasks I have a need for. For blending, I use two main Rake brushes, one is a 1/4 Rake and the other (either-or) a 1/8 or 1/4 Angular Rake, usually both are at hand. These give us a wide surface area, and when rotated 90 degrees, a thin linear edge for many useful strokes. Overall, depending on how many oils paints I'm using I try to have a #2 brush for each color group (ie. one brush for the browns, greens, orange/yellows. etc.), and one each of the blending brushes.

The thinner used is always *Odorless Turpentine*. It is of a higher quality than straight enamel thinner. I'll keep it simple and stick to this recommendation, again brand matters, use *502 Abt.* or *AK Interactive* (or the top art store brands like *Winsor & Newton*) thinners. When using thinner, the best results are achieved when *you unload the brush onto a paper towel after you dip it in the thinner*. For most successful OPR uses, the blending brush is fundamentally 99% dry and has only a hint of thinner remaining in it. The reason for this is the moment you add too much thinner the oils immediately turn into a wash and flow away, which is counter to the type of effects we are after.

The actual process of applying the oil paint and then blending it out is very straightforward. In fact, it is exactly that simple -- apply the oil color desired to the model, and then blend it in. Where this combines with the HS chipping process is at this moment in the weathering process. Sitting before you on the bench is the painted model with the various marks on the surface created from the painting efforts, and let this be your guide for what oil colors to use and how much to render for each area. Remember the definition of "render" is to provide maximum visual information to the viewer, so working with your road map follow along the details of that particular section and flesh it out with the oils.

All of this effort was designed to break myself out of the mold of what was becoming a rather routine set of processes that could (and was) easily lead our projects down the road of sameness. I was seeing this in my own work, and those of others, and I think it is healthy for us to evaluate and readdress such issues over time. For me growth is an important element of doing what I do, and I recognize that no every modeler is of the same ilk. Thus, my goals with this, as the author, is to simply express these new ideas and then let you absorb and decide if it is something you want to add them into your own arsenal of tools.

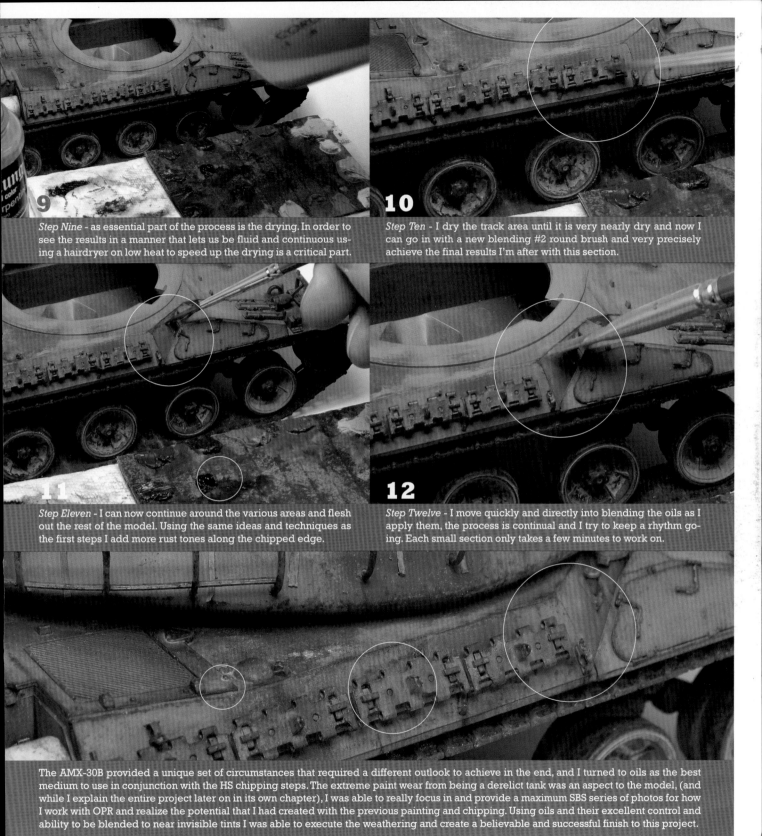

9

Step Nine - as essential part of the process is the drying. In order to see the results in a manner that lets us be fluid and continuous using a hairdryer on low heat to speed up the drying is a critical part.

10

Step Ten - I dry the track area until it is very nearly dry and now I can go in with a new blending #2 round brush and very precisely achieve the final results I'm after with this section.

11

Step Eleven - I can now continue around the various areas and flesh out the rest of the model. Using the same ideas and techniques as the first steps I add more rust tones along the chipped edge.

12

Step Twelve - I move quickly and directly into blending the oils as I apply them, the process is continual and I try to keep a rhythm going. Each small section only takes a few minutes to work on.

The AMX-30B provided a unique set of circumstances that required a different outlook to achieve in the end, and I turned to oils as the best medium to use in conjunction with the HS chipping steps. The extreme paint wear from being a derelict tank was an aspect to the model, (and while I explain the entire project later on in its own chapter), I was able to really focus in and provide a maximum SBS series of photos for how I work with OPR and realize the potential that I had created with the previous painting and chipping. Using oils and their excellent control and ability to be blended to near invisible tints I was able to execute the weathering and create a believable and successful finish to this project.

PIGMENT APPLICATION

PIGMENTS

The third main element in my weathering regime is the mighty pigments. In my opinion, nothing replicates earth effects better than these excellent dedicated modeling products. It's one of the reasons I truly love to model armor, being able to recreate realistic dust, dirt and mud is all part of the fun and pigments bring this home for us.

By now I suspect most of you are familiar with the popular brands on the market and I have used the ones produced from *MIG Productions* for most of my modeling career. While I know this is one-sided, to be fair to the other great products available they all work in basically the same manner and share the same general results. With that said, there are a lot of new pigments for sale and I'm very happy to see them proliferate in the hobby. I'll be using more of the other newer brands moving forward too.

My preferred application process is almost always to apply them dry, then add a liquid fixer to set them in place. My two favorite fixers are *Tamiya's X-20A* acrylic thinner, which works great for most general dust and dirt effects, and for a stronger bond on thicker dried mud, I switch to a dedicated fixer such as the one from *MP*, appropriately called *Pigment Fixer. AK Interactive* has also introduced a great new fixer as well, and they both offer the strength to handle any deeper and thicker mud applications.

When I use pigments wet, it is usually for flicking on wet mud splatters and other similar effects. And for stains and wet looks in the mud itself, I like to add as much oil and pigment effect products as I can. Between oil paints and the various wet effects products available we can recreate nearly any wet or moist earth effect you can think of.

PIGMENT APPLICATION

When I work with pigments, I never use just one color. I have learned from years of experience that

thoughts on the power of pigments:

• nothing replicates the wide variety of earth effects better than pigments, and their working range is expansive from light dust to heavy mud, wet or dry. The trick to achieving success from this wide envelope is determined largely by the ratio of pigment to fixer. For obvious reasons, dust applications require much less fixer and using an airbrush is a great way to apply the fixer in a misting style to set the dust in place. To create the dried caked-on mud seen above, a much thicker pigment layer is carefully set with more fixer so the pigments take on a true wet look and then they are dried rapidly with a hairdryer (on low heat), cracking them as they dry. From there, adding a myriad of stains into the surface (usually by flicking wet oil or enamel washes) is an effective method to add even more grittiness to the end results.

I use a straight forward application process and take my pigment mixture with a large brush apply a layer of pigments on the horizontal surfaces. Placing the model horizontal allows gravity to work for us, and from here I set them in place with a liquid fixer like *X-20A* thinner.

The ability to add a host of stains and various other effects into the pigments both dry and wet is a powerful element to the finishing process. The use of enamels and oils is preferred so that they do not disturb the pigments or the acrylic paint underneath.

The end result is some of the most realistic earthen effects possible, far greater than what pastels can achieve. By including a broad range of colors in the pigments we can add a level of visual depth and represent a wide variety of dust, dirt and mud type finishes.

we can achieve a much more interesting and realistic result from the pigments by creating "batches" of colors to give superior depth to final effects. They are essentially paint pigments and thus can be mixed just as easily. To do this, I use 35mm film containers because of the airtight lids and make bathes of three ranges for each project; a light, medium and dark range of colors. Once you make a series of batches you can then reuse them and simply add other colors to modify their tone for each new project. In this manner, the pigments tend to last a very long time and this becomes a more efficient and effective application process. When I apply the colors, I always work light to dark and for the common lower hull side area, top to bottom as well. This will illustrate how the wetter earth accumulates on the lower regions of the vehicle.

The two main types of applicators for the fixer is either a large round brush (usually old and worn out), or an eye dropper for heavier wetter applications. The crucial tip to effectively applying the fixer is to use capillary action and let the liquid be pulled into the pigments. You want to carefully touch the areas around the pigments and let the fixer flow out of the brush or dropper and be absorbed into the dry pigments, watching the flow and gauging how much fixer is going on. I try to keep the relative amount of fixer even throughout the process. And by altering the ratio of pigments and fixer quantities you can create a variety of effects.

Once the pigments are wet, I use a hair dryer and carefully dry them off, ready for the stain applications if required. Staining pigments is very easy and extremely effective means to up the level of realism in them. I rarely just sign off on the pigments once they are dry, I routinely add as much stains as possible to model. For this I use all available products such as oils, washes and pre-made wet and grime effects, all of which will give good results. Applying stains is also very easy, I use both direct application with a brush to place the stain exactly where I want, such as a suspension joint, and/or via flicking to add the random element to the equation. I usually overlap these effects and continually apply my layering concept throughout the process.

D9R ARMORED DOZER(USMC)

1/35 Varja Miniatures D9R Armored Dozer (USMC)

Armored D9R Dozer   ●

I want to believe inside each of us lies a kid at heart that is absolutely fascinated with large construction equipment. Militarize such beasts and for those of us of like mind we are in modeling heaven. By the time you read this, there will be a new-tool 1/35 injected molded kit on the market of this particular subject from *MENG Models*. A brand new 1/35 D9R Armored Dozer! And we know the feeling is that it's a must build; no two ways around it, building what is arguably the coolest kit today will surely be pure modeling joy.

For me though, I had to work with the *Varja Miniatures* resin kit and that, while cool too, was a very different experience to what the *MENG* kit will provide. Not good or bad, just different. In the way resin can be. And what results from the construction was for me one of the most interesting canvases to paint in a long time. By this time, I had developed my use of the *Hairspray Technique* to a very high level and I knew I wanted to exploit this method to it's absolute maximum performance. I knew the type of weathering I was after and there was one true path to get there. While the construction is easily much more involved than the new plastic kit, the painting process if you chose a similar scheme is essentially the same. Thus the timing of this chapter to the real world market is ideal.

And like all great projects, it starts with the research and finding those just right photos necessary to create the final landscape. And find I did, thanks to the proliferation of images from the two Gulf Wars, I found the perfect candidate for my weathering experiment from the USMC.

D9R ARMORED DOZER

CONSTRUCTION

Sometimes a project will come across your path that is a must build. It has that unique quality that you feel will make it stand above the rest of your models -- that X-factor element. Caterpillar's impressive D9 series bulldozer is an absolute beast of a vehicle in the civilian world and once it was militarized, it becomes even more so. It's sheer size and bulk would translate to a very substantial model in 1/35 and *Varja Miniatures* introduced a resin kit of the Armored D9R version as used by both the IDF and US military, which proved to capture the visceral appeal of the real thing.

Modern resin kits are definitely an improvement over resin kits from the 80's and 90's and here the resin was, by and large, crisp and cleanly cast in a neutral gray resin that was of a fairly low odor content as well. Working with this kit was an overall pleasant experience and in the occasional few spots where the casting was too flawed to fix (I had some large parts that were beyond repair), I returned them back to *Varja Miniatures* and found their customer service was on par with modern companies too. While I was waiting on their replacement, I had some time to ponder the paint scheme and also how to maximize the kit's potential.

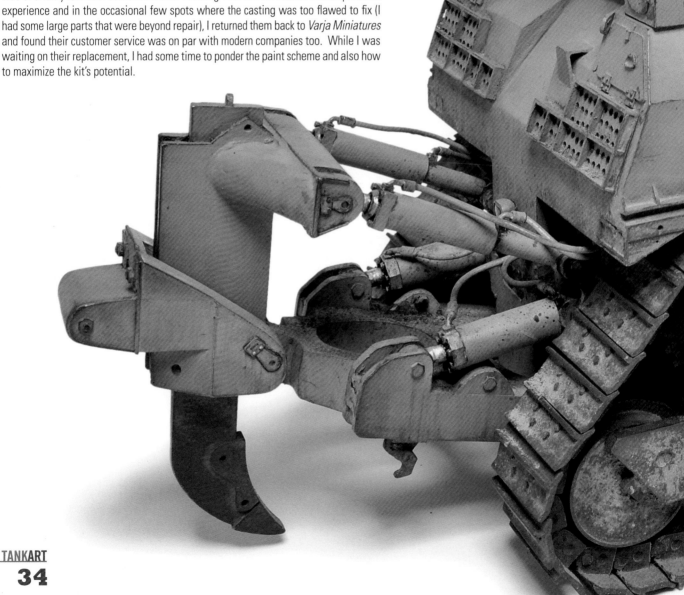

thoughts on how I wanted this model to turn out (my planning notes):

• this was a major project the moment it was announced and I knew I was going to build it. Both the sheer size and the vehicle's intended use meant I was going to be required to give an all-out effort to elevate my game to match the prominence of the model. It started with some good reference photos I found online, one in particular showcased an USMC version with multiple colors and heavy weathering, the perfect choice. To get there I also knew ahead of time I was going to rely heavily on the HS technique to execute the chipped and scratched paintjob correctly, and from there I was going to push my OPR use and pigments to new levels. I'll get into those details and thought processes in greater depth, but this triple course of action was an efficient and successful recipe to ensure maximum success at each step of the process.

Resin kits can fall into the trap of oversimplification due to the complex nature of casting large parts and certain areas would require additional detailing to make them both more accurate and flesh out the necessary look found in these spots -- namely the myriad of missing cables, and hydraulic lines found on the original. Some minor scratchbuilding with basic styrene and small tubing would be called upon to set things right, including some minor casting flaws too. I also took the time to replace the metal tubes of the four large main hydraulic arms that actuate the large dozer blade up front. Here I used real aluminum rods the same diameter as the resin parts, with the added benefit of making the blade workable versus it's fixed placement using the resin parts.

The bulk of the kit assembles without too much drama, dry fitting is the most important task to do with resin and this one proved no different. The top armored cab would require a few sandings to create a quality mating surface with the top of the large lower hull. This was one of the critical joints because the interior would need to be painted beforehand and then the large superstructure could be sealed up. That, and the armored glass, which required some creative thinking to paint correctly.

TRACK UPGRADE

Outside of those factors, the last hurdle on this kit were the tracks. While they are single cast link-to-link tracks, the fit left a lot to be desired. CAT tracks are always taut and fit snugly, and to get these to respond properly, I found a good solution was to drill out the fixed track pin holes and fit each link together with a proper track pin using styrene rod matched to size. This did the trick and removed the slop between the track links, giving them the right look.

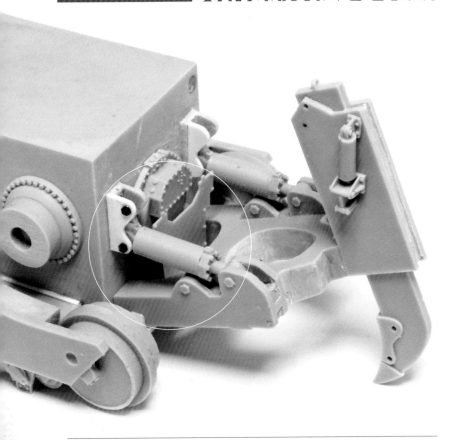

Certain areas like this bracket required replacement parts scratchbuilt from styrene.

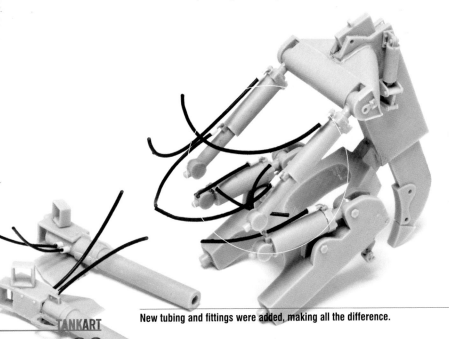

New tubing and fittings were added, making all the difference.

targeting flaws and then adding solutions:

• resin kits are unique in that they are mostly created using individual master molds and normally cast by hand (in the overall sense, this is not a factory manufactured effort like injected molded kits). Thus, casting flaws are routine and knowing how to fix them goes a long way to success. Air bubbles are filled with CA glue, and warped parts are reheated.

• for larger parts that have excessive air bubbles or warped surfaces (the two major flaws), there are other options to fix them. Sometimes it is also simply easier to scratchbuild your own, as in the case of some brackets found on the rear of the hull. Air bubbles are filled with CA glue and accelerator, and warped parts can be gently heated and re-straightened on a flat surface while they cool down.

thoughts on *Varja Miniatures* resin D9 kit:

• Overall, the *Varja* resin kit of this monster is a stout base platform from which to make a world class model. *MENG's* new 1/35 plastic kit is obviously going to be the new go to kit, but life is to be had with this kit. And once built up, it looks the part and provides fantastic painting and weathering opportunities. Minor details like the tubing and the new track pins go a long way to adding the right improvements.

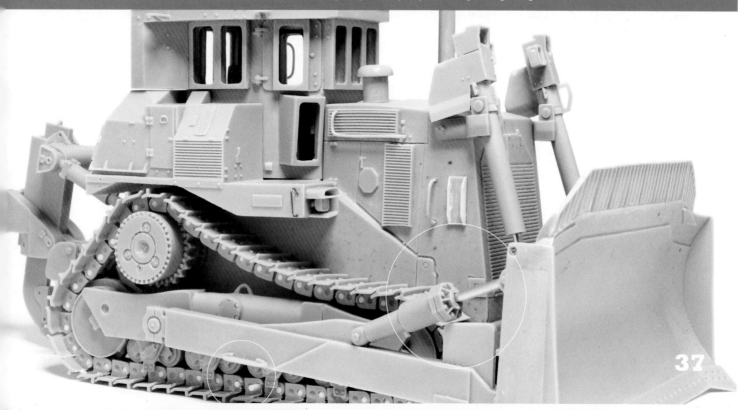

paint callouts for the Armored D9 project:

- **1st layer - RUST UNDERCOAT:** The initial pre-shading paint layer is created from *Lifecolor's Rust & Dust Diorama* paint set.

- **2nd layer - CAT YELLOW:** This unique color was created from mixing *Tamiya XF-3 Flat Yellow* and a few drops of *X-26 Clear Orange*, which gives it a slight glossy sheen.

- **3rd layer - SAND CAMO:** The main Sand color is a tricky color to get right. Nothing out of the bottle worked for me so I mixed *XF-20 Medium Grey*, *XF-57 Buff*, and *XF-55 Deck Tan*, keeping a hint of gray to the color.

- **4th layer - GREEN CAMO:** I used straight *XF-5 Flat Green* for the USMC shade.

quick ref:
- RUST BASE:
  Lifecolor Rust set

- CAT YELLOW:
  XF-3 Flat Yellow
  X-26 Clear Orange

- SAND CAMO:
  XF-20 Med. Grey
  XF-57 Buff
  XF-55 Deck Tan

- GREEN BASE:
  XF-5 Flat Green

PAINTING BEGINS

Heading into this paintjob I had to stay focused on how I wanted to arrive at the desired end result. Having selected a great photo of an USMC D9R, which showcased a heavily weathered paintjob and worn away in the lower areas revealing layers of metal, rust, yellow and the top camouflage. All of which makes sense because these dozers were shipped from the CAT facilities and started life in the famous yellow color.

But it is so much more than that. Additional D9R dozer photos illustrated the depth to this type of paint wear, going down to the metal in multiple areas and with a voracity not normally seen on a regular combat vehicle. Rust plays an important part as well, so I had to set up the right plan to utilize the HS technique to it's fullest advantage. I knew going in what I wanted to do, now I had to simply execute this plan. As if that was not enough to work out, there are two other key areas that needed attention before anything could happen -- 1) painting of

Stage One - the subassemblies are all primed in my favorite Mr. Surfacer.

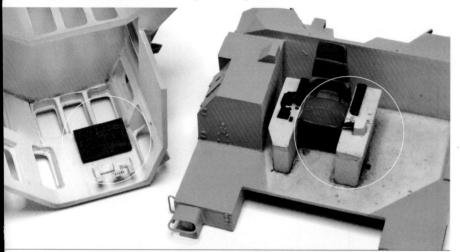

Stage Two - the sparse interior is painted in off-white with subtle weathering applied.

Stage Three - the tint for the armored glass panels was applied to the edges only.

the interior and 2) the armored glass panels before I could seal the superstructure up for the exterior painting. Compared to the *MENG* D9R, the *Varja* kit is lacking details in its interior. In fact, it is missing quite a bit and frankly it was too much for me to update at the time given the limited visibility thru the windows. Thus, I gave the interior its due diligence in the correct colors, added some dirt and stains to the floor and turned my attention to solving the armored glass issue.

The glass in the kit is clear resin pieces, and the real stuff has a strong blue-green tint to it. I studied some of what aircraft modelers do when confronted with tinted windscreens and then tried a few ideas to see what worked best. My first thought was to simply spray a thin film of clear blue-green tint on the back side, but they became foggy, so after I cleaned them off, I decided to paint the edges only with a mix of *Tamiya X-23 Clear Blue* and *X-25 Clear Green*. This worked well in that it kept the clear areas "clear", and lent a strong tint to each piece.

EXTERIOR PAINTING

With the interior and glass ready, I could then close up the hull and mask off the windows and proceed with all haste to the exterior paintjob. Something I was itching to get to! I determined the heavily exposed rust layers are the most important visual element on this model's finish, so I started the painting with a solid layer of dark gray to both pre-shade the model and provide me with a "dark metal" color I knew would be the exposed metal areas from the

39

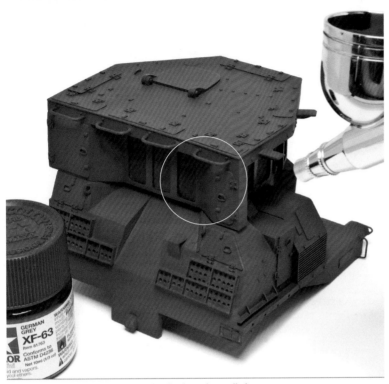

The base metal tone is the first shade of paint to be applied.

The first layer of HS is applied, and then the dark rust tones, ready for the next step.

chipping. A lot of wear and tear was planned, so I utilized *Tamiya XF-63 German Grey* thinned with Lacquer Thinner for this step to ensure I had the strongest bond possible.

HAIRSPRAY & RUST - ROUND 1

The next step was the start of the rust layers. Here I really had to ensure I created some depth to the rust tones, they would be very visible and would make or break this project. First up was to apply two even layers of HS over the entire model. I find it best to have the model entirely covered in HS even if I don't work certain areas, because it's when you don't have it applied in that "spot" is often when you will chip it and wish that you did. From there I spray a dark brown rust color using *Tamiya XF-79 Linoleum Deck Brown*, this time thinned with water and sprayed in light thin coats to build up the paint slowly. Note, I did not spray the entire model in the dark brown, just those areas that I felt were beneficial during the chipping.

The next step was by far the most important in regards to how I laid down the tones and created the visual texture to the rust. Some of the best rust paints today are those from the fantastic *Lifecolor Rust & Dust Diorama Set*. I've used them multiple times on my projects and their versatility and results have never let me down.

The rust application process was therefore a bit more unique on this project, in fact, getting it correct was paramount to success. The *LC* Rust paints are quite like a liquid

thoughts on the using control:

• to date, I've had a lot of experience creating finishes with the HS technique and as I gained the practice and knowledge of its strengths and weaknesses I can implement it with more control and precision. I had factored a total of five individual rounds of layered chipping necessary to create the final look on the D9R, and with the stage set it was a rather straightforward challenge to get each layer to do what I wanted it to do.

• one of the main elements of success with the HS technique, and many others for that matter, is knowing how much quantity of each product to apply. This is what is meant with control, and to a certain extent subtlety. A lot of what I talk about is underwritten with the simple fact I am always applying each step in a controlled and refined manner. Even when I want a lot of randomness to my finish, such as with the splattered rust layers shown at right, it was not created is some crazy haphazard manner. I apply each step with restraint as I build up the tones I ultimately want. Thin layers will always lead to a greater path of success. Avoid thick single applications in almost everything we do.

pigment and provide a nice matte finish and subtle texture, and I decided to use small sponges as applicators and a toothbrush to provide the randomness you get by flicking the bristles. As you can see in the photos, I did a lot of work with this 4-color Rust paint system and built up the paints from light to dark, dabbing on thinned layers in a translucent fashion to create the various tones. I completed the process with some toothbrush flicking to create the spots of dark rust, which adds that final touch to the finish.

HS + CAMO PAINTING

With the model starting to look the part, the bulk of the real painting effort was about to begin. The rust tone foundation being the building blocks to layer upon, and from here I started the multiple applications of hairspray and camo paint. The first color I applied, (while not really camouflage), is the famous CAT Yellow, which is a mixture of *Tamiya XF-3 Flat Yellow* and a few drops of *X-26 Clear Orange* that

thoughts on embracing this project's challenge: ●

• this was a major project for me, and with the 1/35 *MENG* kit out now, I imagine anything similar will also be a large involved project for any of you too. The D9's are large complicated vehicles no matter the type of kit or scale. Thus, I approached my processes intending this model to be one of the best results I could possibly achieve and not compromise myself with that goal, meaning not cut it short to make a show, or other deadline. I wanted a maximum effort on my part, to truly push myself to the next level and see what I could achieve. Here I wanted to prove to myself the training and experience that I had gained these past few years with certain ideas could indeed provide proven results in the real world. I personally don't believe I could have pulled off this finish without reliance on certain methods that are now common to my finishes, so to get to the final level I was after I had to dive in with both feet and not look back. Those decisions *had* to be made up front and with eyes wide open.

• naturally, commitment to a project at this level is not without it's consequences and the style of breakdown for the subassembly construction process required for the painting steps added considerable effort to the overall completion time frame. Plus, the fact it's simply a very big model, no two ways about it. All in all this was the most involved modeling project I have yet undertaken and with such risks comes greater rewards.

The rust layers were applied with the *LC Rust* paints, small sponges and a toothbrush.

Once the rust layers were applied, I sprayed HS and then the CAT Yellow...it's ready for the chipping.

The results of the HS chipping efforts on the first round of yellow over the rust tones.

tips on the HS chipping: •

• I explain in greater detail the HS chipping in the previous technique chapter, which showcases the D9 as well, (and also in the first two **TANKART** volumes). To expand on those fundamental ideas, it is important to note on a model like this whereby the effects had to look realistic for success, I studied a lot of reference photos before and during the process. That included walking around construction sites to look at actual equipment up close to see how the marks look in person and the subtle directional elements at play.

• the direction of the marks, the size and volume of them in certain areas, the asymmetrical differences in sections and where the marks stop and start are all studied and implemented from reference photos and my own personal observations. That was exciting to be able to do this process because we have amazing 1:1 references in action today that are most relevant to this project. The success of this project hinged on these critical steps in the painting process.

My choice the final layer of CARC sand camo was a blend of *Tamiya* acrylics, and I went with a grayish tone often scene after the vehicles are on site for some time.

thoughts on the many shades of US military paint shades for desert armor:

• from the modeler's perspective we often strive to balance what is actual with what we can interpret for our own project's needs. As is often the case, there is no 100% right or wrong rule with paints; history has continually shown us the most strict paint mixtures from the factory can vary from vehicle to vehicle, and this is magnified when the elements of combat and weather are combined. Colors, to me, are representatives of the subject and I strive for a shade I can work with and look "right" to my eye. This often requires making my own colors, since out of the bottle paint colors are sometimes too strict for my tastes. But that is what makes the hobby interesting, we always have choices.

Interpreting the many colors at work is as much art as it is science. My simple guide is my eye, does it look "right" in-scale? I judge most of my colors on this basic premise.

gives a slight semi-gloss sheen with a hint of orange in the yellow to match the color better. After which I then spend a lot of time, very slowly and carefully chipping the yellow back to show the various rust layers underneath. This is probably the most important round of chipping because it will dictate where the subsequent marks will go as I continue to build up the paint layers. And to emphasis the process I am studying my references closely to see where the marks should be going.

Once that is done I can proceed to the first real layer of camo, the CARC Sand color. I must mention here that I do not seal the model prior to the next application of HS because I have learned it is an unnecessary step because I am very subtle with my marks, and once an area is already gone over with water, the chances of a lot more chips occurring is greatly diminished. I know where I am going to chip the next layer, and this keeps everything in check. If you want to seal with a varnish for extra security please do so, but I wanted to clarify that is not normally part of my process. With that said, I proceed with the HS and sand paint. Again, I stick with *Tamiya* paints and create my own mixture from *XF-20 Medium Grey*, *XF-57 Buff*, and *XF-55*

The engine panels of this USMC unit was left in green, or replaced at some point in time.

thoughts on focusing on special areas:

• on nearly every model, I try to find one special area that receives more attention to create a focal point of interest that both brings the viewer in closer, and then directs them elsewhere. On the D9, I used the USMC green panels to be this element. The green engine panels catch your eye, and then as you get in closer you are drawn the to the green paint on the back of the dozer blade. This subconscious manipulation is what creates a top caliber model. You want to move the viewer around and keep their interest going so they fully immersed in the model before them. Not every model has such properties and this is part of our challenge as the artist to incorporate such areas without looking forced, or overdone.

The green along with myriad of chipping and scratches creates a strong area of visual interest and really adds to the final look of the model.

Deck Tan leaning towards a grayer tone for the final color. I also take more time to build up the opacity of the top coat to create an authentic look, leaving just the areas of chipping with less paint to facilitate the process. Once dry, I take my time and carry on with the chipping to illustrate the layered effects seen in the photos.

From here, I repeated the HS application, this time with the green areas on the two engine panels and the back of the dozer blade. These sections were then chipped to create the final look of the painted surfaces. All in all, the HS work was done over the course of 2-3 weeks, I went very slowly and kept my patience up so as not to rush anything. In the end, I was very pleased with the results and this led me right to the next major part of the process, switching to the oil paints.

OPR - utilizing the oil paints was essential to giving the multi-layered paint the right patina and finish.

tips for using the painted effects to guide us to success with the oil paint rendering:

• up to this point everything I was doing was with acrylic paints. What happens from this effort is what can be called a "road-map for the weathering". One of the tricks that really allows for maximum success is to utilize what the painted areas are giving us as a guide to expand the weathering. What I mean by this is all of those wonderful chips and scratches I did with the HS technique are going to be my map of where I am going to use the oils to further enhance each section. The hard word is already done. At this stage, simply following along the surface with the oils to bring out the richness in the paint, add the grime and shadows into the surface, and in general bring the metal to life so it looks like the real vehicle is part of the process of using the previous efforts to guide us along to the final results.

• over the course of my work, with the introduction of oil paints as a significant product that I use on every project I had an epiphany about where I was going with my projects. What was transpiring in my head was the reality that OPR could ultimately replace the filter and wash steps completely, I was less and less inclined to believe I *must* do those steps all the time. You might have already asked yourself this question "where are the filter and pinwash pages?", and you would be correct, they are not here in this chapter. What has happened in my more recent work is that I am starting to reduce those steps, sometimes removing them all together, and simply going straight into the OPR stages.

• I do this for the primary reasons of being more efficient with my processes, (filters in particular were becoming redundant for me), and to add a greater degree of control and creativity to the finish. Pinwashes are designed to follow the details of the surface, whereas with an OPR pinwash type of effect I can move beyond it to create more original results and this elevates the model to another level and in the end breaks the form that all of my models will look the same over time. This was a critical realization for me, I had been searching for the right approach to avoid the problem of my models becoming overly repetitive, and this finally came to be when I embraced the effects I could achieve using the oil paints.

I worked the engine deck and exhaust details with additional white mapping.

OPR ONLY

In the orange boxes on these pages I am opening up the discussion on some of my newer thoughts about weathering, and the processes at work. On this model, I truly began to embrace the concept I could realistically achieve the bulk of the paint weathering solely with oils and forego the usual filter and pinwash steps. Up to this point, I had toyed around with the idea to see if it was indeed feasible and the results worth pursuing. After some experimenting on a test model, I liked the results, so I decided to incorporate this new concept into the D9R's finish.

It all starts with the cardboard palette. This is a crucial step to ensure the oils perform as intended, and here I chose a limited color spectrum to work with the shades of tans, rust, yellows and earth tones, which I would use to show general wear and tear and the paint fading, in lieu of the filters. I always have a spectrum of dark tones too, and these would replace the pinwash steps in essence.

With that setup in place, I have my selection of brushes in hand, and usually one in my mouth too since it makes a great third hand sometimes, and I start in one small section of the model and begin the OPR process. Like I mention earlier, the road map for the weathering is already done for me with my HS chipping, and I simply start applying the color I want on each mark to bring it out more. I use the yellow, orange and light tans to work the sand camo color and CAT Yellow areas, the richer browns for the rust tones, and then the dark colors are used to enhance the panel lines, illustrate the grimy areas and bring out the darker rust and metal tones.

I work my way around the major subassemblies of the project until I have tackled the entire model. Again, like the HS chipping, this is slow going and requires patience to achieve the desired results. I couldn't rush this process at all, which pays rewards later on. Any mistakes are easily dealt with because oils are so forgiving, and remember to make use of both streaking brush strokes and stippling to create the various special effects. As I move up the model,

• the combination of the three main processes of HS chipping paint layers, OPR weathering, and pigments is the essence of this project. Because of the nature of what a bulldozer does, each step plays a critical role for success. With the OPR elements completed, working the pigments to achieve the desired finish was the last piece of this puzzle, maybe even the most vital one.

• color selection is important and I wanted the tones to work with the overall scheme of the model and not fight it, or overwhelm it either. I created my pigments in batches of light, medium and dark tones and like so much of what I do, I apply them from light to dark in an effort to layer up the earth in the same manner as the rest of the model. I generally start with a light layer to set the dustier tones down, I set the model on its side so each surface is horizontal, I apply the pigments dry, then set them in place with the fixer. I used both *Tamiya X-20A* thinner and *MIG Prod. Pigment Fixer* for the heavier layers. I do not use very much fixer, just enough to get the surface wet and by playing with various ratios of how much pigments are applied to the surface followed by the fixer I could create various textures. I strongly recommend you test out this idea on a test model to see how they perform.

I use less and less colors since the sand camo reacts dramatically and everything must be kept in control and look balanced.

PIGMENTS

Developing the paint weathering with just the oils was a great way to bring forth the maximum value within the paintjob, but to truly get the model to a level of weathering I was after, switching to pigments was the only option left to do. I knew in my head I wanted to contrast the heavy earth layers against the cleaner upper superstructure and it started with making the light, medium and dark pigment mixtures from *MIG Productions* pigments. I based the colors mostly around *European Dirt*, and then added similar tones leaning heavier on the lighter shades for the light tone such as *Beach Sand* and *Industrial Earth*, and the opposite of the darkest shade with *Dark Mud* and *Russian Earth*.

This gives the pigments maximum depth and I start by applying the lightest shade first. As I describe, the model is turned on it's side so the working surface is horizontal, the pigments are put in place, then the fixer is added using a brush and some capillary action to pull the liquid into the pigments. It's important not to touch them after, and only with some intentional strokes, such as the downward streaks I applied while they are drying.

I stained the pigments with a plethora of oil stains, flicked from the end of a brush for random effects.

To create the streaked pigments, carefully use a fan brush and thinner to pull them downward as they dry. Caution: it does not take much effort!

tips for creating various textures: ●

• pigments provide us with a remarkable level of textures, but it takes some experience to get the right look in-scale. The majority of the time, the model needs to be propped up so the working surface is horizontal and gravity holds the dry pigments in place as we add the fixer to it.

• typically it works best to do it all in one go, then if more is needed to make greater texture simply repeat the process. I had to do this on the sponsons and the face of the dozer blade.

• when applying the pigments, do not brush them onto the surface, instead use a tapping motion on the pigment brush and let them fall into place. Hold the brush a few inches over the surface, not too high so they fall where you intend them to go. Do not breath on them after!

49

The tracks are repinned with styrene rods to create a much tighter fit.

The first layer of paint is a dark steel gray used for the base.

Rust tones are created with the Lifecolor Rust paints and applied with sponges and heavily thinned paint layered up. The sponges create a random finish.

The tracks are finished with pigments applied in thin layers.

thoughts on applying pigments on tracks: ●

• there is usually not too much difference when applying pigments to the tracks vs. the rest of the model, but you can control the application to create different looks. It will always look more realistic to add the pigments in a variety of patterns in order to break up the links so they do not look too repetitive.

• also work each track run slightly different, or dramatically different if the look you want calls for it. Asymmetrical results can be fun and more interesting on the final model.

• like the model, I apply the pigments dry then add the fixer to set them in place. Once dry, I often flick oil stains along the length of the run to add a grittier appearance. Also, altering the ratio of pigments to fixer will result in different looks and texture, and here I used more fixer and less pigments to create the tracks at left.

• evaluating the project at various stages of the process is always a great way to ensure things are going how you hoped. While it is important to remain flexible with the weathering so as not to force it too much, keeping things natural, there is room to maneuver and alter anything not to your liking. For example, once the tracks were mounted it becomes hard to see all of the pigment work along the hull sides, so I have to think about where do I need to do more, or if some areas are good enough not disturb them too much. The tracks really change the look of the dozer and become such a focal point because they are so visible and not hidden, so I make sure to finish them off properly with graphite to show polished metal areas, which contrast with the matte rust and pigments. I would also start to add more and more grime to the sides and grease stains on the moving parts to arrive at a balance of weathering I was happy with.

D9R ARMORED DOZER

The fit of the tracks was important because the track sag had to look correct, which of course was why I chose to re-pin each link. This worked out great in the end and the tension was vastly improved. I'd expect the *MENG* kit to be a big improvement here, and maybe we will even see a set of *Friulmodel* tracks in the future.

thoughts on building up the layers of heavy weathering:

• I have spoken a lot about *layering* in the previous **TANKART** volumes, I talk so much about the relevance and importance this concept has to the final outcome of a project, and on this model it was no different. The D9R required layer upon layer of pigments and oil stains to arrive at the end game. For me this is probably the most enjoyable part of the weathering processes; the constant analysis of the results and the overall balance of the project whilst I move it along with each addition to the finish. It can be very therapeutic in the tinkering of the myriad of weathering details I attend to. I will continually manipulate the weathering, work with the oils and add the stains as I seek the ultimate finish. The trick is to keep the changes small, subtle and do not make large dramatic fixes to anything. Often times the model will not come together until the final 10% of the effort, so it must remain in the back of your head to be patient, stay the course and keep working at it.

To create those streaks, once the pigments are wet and drying, you can set the model upright, use a clean rake brush and then carefully pull the pigments downward using the fewest strokes possible. The more you touch the worse it will get, so try to do each streak in one stroke per width of the brush.

DOZER BLADE

The main focus however, was to be on the large dozer blade. I knew if I nailed this element, the model would be a true success. But I wanted a very specific look to the pigments with thick caked-on mud and cracked earth effects. To do this step properly, I first practiced on a test model to see approximately how much pigments were needed and how much fixer is necessary to make it work. With that experience, I made some subtle application changes to my usual process for this part...I start with a misting layer of *Pigment Fixer* from the airbrush to give the smooth blade surface some added grip, then I drop substantial amounts of

The pigments are worked along the upper areas where the crew frequent to tie the model together.

Final details on the tracks and chips were to go over them with some graphite, which imparts a realistic metallic look to each area.

The ripper is next to be fitted after the tracks are on. I added the fittings and hydraulic hoses to the ripper, which made a major difference in the details.

The main hydraulic cylinders were painted with *Gunze* burnishing metal paint.

tips on detailing the ripper:

• the *Varja* kit is lacking obvious details in a few critical areas, the main one being no hydraulic pressure lines are present on the prominent rear ripper. This could not go without correction, so I used a combination of scale rubber tubing and scratchbuilt styrene end connectors. Reference images are plenty, so it was very straightforward update to this kit. Again, I expect with the *MENG* kit available this will be a non-issue if you choose that route.

• projects such as this one really do require complete attention to detail from start to finish. So much potential is contained in a subject like this that truly mixes two genres into one, I knew when the kit came my way I had to go 100% in each area to unlock the beauty contained within, well as much as us modelers will find and term beautiful! To achieve that level of painting and weathering detail, each section must be gone over multiple times to both create the right depth of weathering, and scale refinement to create the final look *in-scale*, which is the true challenge of all our models. The combination of the HS technique, the OPR weathering and pigments have now become the cornerstones by which I can control and manipulate the finished project.

The tracks still fought me a little and one connection in particular was a bit wonky when I took the photos. These issues can sometimes slip by even the most vigilant modeler.

pigments on top utilizing all three main shades layered up from light to dark.

Once I was comfortable the quantity, I started to add the fixer straight with an eye-dropper touching all the edges around the perimeter of the blade so the pigments would absorb the fixer evenly. I used more fixer on this application so the pigments took on a wetter look, and using the hair dryer on low heat, and holding it farther away, about 8-10" or so, I very gently start to dry the pigments, being careful not to disturb them during the process. Once they start to get dry, you can see this happening, I switch to my brushes and with some dark oil paints flick a bunch on stains onto the drying pigments, randomly touching certain areas to create dark wetter patches to the earth effects. After all of this effort I finalize the drying with the hairdryer and because of the added volume of fixer the pigments take on the hard dry caked-on look.

The last bit of pigment work I do is something of a risk (well, greater than usual), and using my hobby knife I carefully pick away a few patches of the dried pigments on the blade to create the hard flaked edges and exposed patches. I see this on the real thing, so I decided to risk it and luckily I was able to pull it off.

With the critical pigments finalized, I could finish the assembly of the blade and carefully fit it into place. Because I had previously substituted the resin hydraulic rods for real metal tubes, there is some limited movement to the blade, which looks more authentic as a result in the photos. The project was essentially completed at this point, and the last thing I had to attend to was the addition of graphite to all of the exposed metal edges around the model, which truly imparts that metallic element to the paint finish and gives it the look true heavy metal. By all accounts, the *Varja Miniatures Armored D9R Dozer* represents one of the true beasts on the battlefield, and it was the same on my workbench too where it tested my skills from start to finish, top to bottom.

The dozer blade weathering is such a major focal point on the model, I knew I had to elevate my game and pull off a fantastic effort with the earth effects. Using a combination of *MIG Productions Pigment Fixer* and their excellent line of pigments, the results came out as intended and took the finished model to a whole new level. It's having such quality products in our hobby that truly allows us to express and expand on our processes to create ever better projects. It is with a ton of pride that this model of the CAT D9R Armored Dozer took Gold at the Euro Militaire show, often considered the most competitive military modeling event.

• How could I elevate both my own skill set and present a final project that would become a piece worthy of discussion? As modelers, we have to balance our egos, our project goals, and our desires on a personal level to strive harder within the deadlines of the real world, whether it is for a show, or an article, or just to have it completed so you can move onto to the next one. Where we draw the line is often as much instinct and subliminal internal evaluations as it is comments from friends and fellow modelers. It's OK to show pride in your work, to share it online or elsewhere because many of us do get that satisfaction from such completed projects, after all we are human. But that also creates a lot of pressure on ourselves, can make the hobby a more stressful endeavor than if we were working in a bubble only for ourselves. And certainly there are many of us that are fine with that, but for those striving for the greater glory remember to breath and exhale on a regular basis to keep it all in perspective and balanced.

57

The final pigments on the dozer blade are the results of adjusting the ratio of pigments and fixer to create the thick dried-on and cracked look to the mud.

●

thoughts on recreating dried mud:

• getting the pigments to look like cracked dried mud requires some changes to the normal routine -- upping the thickness of the pigment layer and then adding the fixer slowly until it looks wet, at which point you want to dry it faster than normal so it begins to crack. I use my hair dryer for so many processes and this one is no different, just take care not to disturb the finish as it dries. I find it best to hold it far away from the surface while the pigments dry.

thoughts on the final composition of the model:

• on a project like this one where the type of vehicle and the way it is used really helps to give us plenty of opportunities to have a ton of visual interest within the painting and weathering, we must still maintain good composition and balance across the model. The front of the blade is balanced by the strong green color heavily chipped, while the expanse of sand camo is broken up with the green engine panels and so on. Working around the model we can then pick out finer and finer details to increase the level of depth within the balance of the overall scheme and presentation. This is where you the author can control the viewer and make their experience greater by bringing them and revealing more layers the closer they get to the model.

The completed and heavily weathered D9R is an impressive beast of a model. It provides all the necessary ingredients to make for a tremendous project.

thoughts on the some lasting overall impression and those remaining details that make the model sing:

• I like to take my time and constantly rotate the model around (I use a small "lazy Suzan" turntable) and ensure I cover each area appropriately. Anything not where I want it, I go back over it with the right process. Because I have had eyes on the project for months, this helps me to see if I can catch a spot I might have missed, or to complete a section I may not have finished 100%. The constant stop and start from such a long project is always a concern, so take the right steps to make certain the model is at least to a point of proper presentation to the public.

Armored D9R Dozer ●

There were no two ways about this project, it was a very important piece for me on so many levels. The subject choice demanded I put my best effort into the finish and my own personal goals and weathering experiments came together into this one large project, literally! But even with the added pressure, I thoroughly enjoyed myself from start to finish, (OK maybe not all the resin issues), but you know what I mean. It is models like this one that we look back upon with fond memories and remember when it came about in the right way.

As I write this chapter, there has been an utterly relentless amount of modern subject injected-molded kits to hit the market this year, including a brand new tool 1/35 Armored D9R from *MENG Models*. We are truly swimming deep into the best era of scale modeling we have ever seen and this simply fuels my own strong desires to keep producing new models and pushing myself to higher limits. The enthusiasm for the hobby is at an all-time high for me, and I suspect for many of you as well. We can't turn our heads and not run into a new kit, whether it is armor or another subject, we are not short on choices!

The point being that we are all heading into a time whereby we have a lot of amazing projects available to us, the level on reference information is also keeping pace and the ability of the internet to connect all the pieces has definitely changed my modeling practices, for the better I believe.

D9R ARMORED DOZER(USMC)

1/35 Varja Miniatures D9R Armored Dozer (USMC)

D9R ARMORED DOZER (USMC)

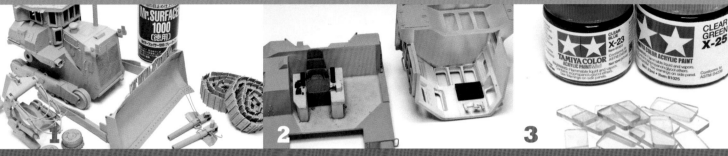

PRIMER

INTERIOR PAINTING

PAINTING THE GLASS

METALLIC BASE COLORS

RUST LAYERS APPLIED

1ST HAIRSPRAY LAYER

YELLOW CHIPPING

BASE SAND CAMO OVER HS

SAND AND GREEN CHIPPING

OIL PAINT RENDERING

OPR

PIGMENT APPLICATION

13 MORE PIGMENT LAYERS

14 TRACK ASSEMBLY

15 BASE TRACK COLOR

16 RUST LAYER APPLIED

17 TRACK PIGMENTS APPLIED

18 TRACKS FITTED

19 WEATHERING CONT.

20 FINAL WEATHERING DETAILS

21 RIPPER FITTED

22 FINAL RIPPER FINISHING

23 BLADE WEATHERED & MOUNTED

24 FINAL WEATHERING DETAILS

RUSSIAN MBT T-62M1 (Afghan)

1/35 Trumpeter T-62 mod. 1972, MIG Prod. T-62M1 conversion

T-62M1 Main Battle Tank

This is a fascinating subject by any stretch of the imagination. Anytime a vehicle survives decades into it's service life to be discovered practically discarded and decaying away in one world's most hostile regions, you know the visual effects are going to be stunning -- in as much a way as a worn out battle tank can be.

Such is the appeal of the now famous (and sadly long gone) Kabul Graveyard. From a modeling perspective, interest is at the very highest of levels. So many dynamic weathering elements can be brought to bear that it begged for the recreation in scale, and doubly good for us from a timing point of view, *Trumpeter* decided to release a brand new tool 1/35 Russian T-62 MBT series; something long overdue in it's own right!

However, that was only half the battle. To really do the subject justice, it had to be the late model T-62M1 adorned in it's bulkier add-on armor package that is still one of the most visually distinctive upgrades fielded, especially the front panels as they curve around the large cast turret shape. Once it was known *Trumpeter* were set to release their new kits, the team at *MIG Productions* set about to introduce the T-62M1 upgrade in all due haste. This was both good and bad, (as I'll discuss later), for our needs it gave us all the parts necessary to recreate one of those relics.

But then that left the task of the paintjob. The allure of all of these abandoned armor vehicles lies in the heavily worn off paint, and there again lies the heart of this project's challenge.

THE CLASSIC PLASTIC & RESIN KITBASH

When I got the call to work on this project I was instantly excited about the possibilities of the finish. On the one hand I knew I was going to get a shot at a brand new kit, which is always a lot of fun and then from my efforts would be able to help sell a new aftermarket set, in this case the *MIG Productions* T-62M1 resin conversion for the new *Trumpeter* 1.35 T-62 Mod. 1972 kit. Cool stuff on both accounts and I was ready to go as soon as the project kits arrived.

MIG Productions resin sets and kits are what I'd call part of the newer generation of castings that are freer from the strong resin odors of the 80's kits and the quality is first rate, often rather amazing on the smaller details. The master was created by the prolific Zackery Sex from Ireland, fans of who will recognize his voracious appetite for all things modern Russian and unique. In fact, it was Zack that contacted me directly to participate in this project. And once I had my hands on the kits, I dove in with as much enthusiasm as they had for the subject. Along with the kit parts I was privy to some special reference photos shot by John Murphy while in Afghanistan, and this was critical to being able to successfully achieve the type of finish we were all after.

But like all good projects, it starts with the construction. Trumpeter has made some good strides in recent years and a lot of their newer releases are far less problematic than their kits of old. While the T-62 series is a huge improvement on the 70's *Tamiya* kit (may it rest in peace), it is not without its faults. That frankly was not a huge surprise given Trumpeter's track record and I watched, like many of you, online how the kit's faults were dissected. Now I take a very pragmatic view on this approach and simply file the information away for

thoughts on painting a realistic multi-layered camo scheme heavily chipped at each layer: ●

• modern armor modelers are very lucky to have such a unique subject as the famous Kabul Graveyard to choose from. The sheer variety of worn-off, peeling and chipped paint is far too captivating to let the chance slip by and not model one of these vehicles. When I sat down and studied the research photos I was sent for this model, I pretty much knew how I was going to tackle it. After the depth of involvement using the Hairspray Technique on the CAT D9R Armored Dozer, I had all the experience required to sit down and lay out how each layer of color was to be applied, and then subsequently worn away, building up to the ultimate result necessary to capture the right look.

I replaced the kit light guard with one made from wire, which I could easily damage.

The weld beads were all made from two-part epoxy that were textured.

later use. I don't get to hung up on a kit's faults and look at what I can affect to the greater good of the project goals that I have. One area I noticed that was both an easy, if not tedious, fix was to add a healthy portion of the kit's missing weld beads that I felt would be necessary. Russian tanks in particular have substantial amount of exterior welding, and the T-62 has a lot. *Trumpeter* forgot just about all of them, so I spent time with that issue.

Another area grossly noticeable are the complete lack of the prominent fuel lines common to the T-55/62 series. *MIG Productions* actually produce a stellar little update set just for this task, which I promptly put to good use. From there I leave the rear dimensional issue alone, and focused the rest of the plastic kit assembly portion on the visual representation of an abandoned and derelict tank, such as empty fender areas, and the exposed exhaust port. The last bit of detailing is the rear engine grille, which I reconstructed from PE mesh and a scratchbuilt styrene frame.

Some good points about the kit are the road wheels and tracks. I found them fairly accurate in detail and even passed over using *Friulmodel* tracks on this project, I liked the kit's late-model RmSH kit tracks that much. I also took advantage of the fact the wheel hubs were separate parts and scratchbuilt an exposed hub often seen on Kabul tanks.

Overall, I enjoyed making these fairly easy corrections and utilized the info flying across the web forums as a general guide to make sure I was on track, and also to know when to hold off and put more energy elsewhere. My penchant to completely correct a kit's faults are nowhere like it used to be, and find that I get more enjoyment from my modeling balancing that process working towards the big picture.

thoughts on the *MP* T-62M1 conversion:

• the actual process of adding the resin parts to the kit were extremely easy and straightforward, actually the perfect starter kitbash for any modeler wanting to try such a conversion.

• the turret is a direct replacement, nothing else required beyond the weld beads I added to the lift rings, otherwise it's a simple drop fit. The nose and belly armor also fit perfectly into place, nothing else required beyond the weld beads as well.

• the initial turret castings were slightly undersized, mine included, and *MP* has since replaced and fixed the issue once it was brought to their attention. They offered a free replacement if you have the original smaller one. Unfortunately, mine was completed after the news was announced, so I have to live with the fact it's not 100% accurate in size. But that's modeling and it can happen on occasion.

thoughts on updating a base kit and making smart improvements:

• the new *Trumpeter* T-62 kits are miles ahead of the ancient *Tamiya* one, but still lack certain details and like many kits have oversized parts. The fenders and support brackets are one such area, even though I chose to keep the stock parts in place. I've already mentioned the missing welds, but otherwise it's a great base to work with regardless of its limited faults. The *MP* resin parts all fit without issue and is about as easy as it gets to make this conversion. The details on the resin parts are also first rate and quite accurate, and once the model was assembled painting could begin straight away, which is why I agreed to work on this project, the challenge of this paintjob was too good to pass by.

The model is now ready for the paintjob. The new resin pieces from *MP* provide a dramatic visual improvement on the stock kit.

73

T-62M1 MAIN BATTLE TANK

paint callouts for the T-62M1 project:

• **1st layer - RUST:** The initial underlying shades of rust, which will show from the HS chipping were sprayed with *Tamiya XF-79 Linoleum Brown* and *XF-3 Flat Yellow* mixed in.

• **2nd layer - GREEN:** This color is the tone of Russian green after it has faded to the very distinct yellow-green shade. I made a custom mix from *Tamiya XF-5 Flat Green, XF-21 Sky* and some *XF-3 Flat Yellow*.

• **3rd layer - CAMO:** there are 3 camo colors oversprayed onto this tank; a light gray, a faded tan, and a very faded black. For these colors I used *Tamiya XF-80 Royal Light Grey, XF-55 Deck Tan,* and *XF-69 NATO Black* respectively. Each of the paint layers was sprayed in very thin layers over a layer of HS for chipping.

quick ref:
• **RUST BASE:**
XF-79 Linoleum Brown
XF-3 Flat Yellow

• **GREEN BASE:**
XF-5 Flat Green
XF-21 Sky
XF-3 Flat Yellow

• **CAMO LAYERS:**
XF-80 Royal Lt. Grey
XF-55 Deck Tan
XF-69 NATO Black

PAINTING BEGINS

It's an understatement to say I was anxious to get to the painting on this project. I have been fascinated with Kabul tanks ever since the first photos appeared online, and once construction was completed I dived right into the paint. As always I primed the model for all the reasons I mention previously, it's a multi-media project and the amount of abuse the paint will receive it adds strength to the paint's adhesion.

When I studied the reference photos, it was clear to me that I was going to maximize the HS technique, very much like the D9 Dozer project. This time though, the results had to more accurately reflect the look of a tank long since abandoned and repainted a number of times in the field, with personnel and equipment probably not commonly used for such tasks. There is a distinct look to these rundown vehicles and my primary goal was to obtain that level of finish. The extreme chipping was very prevalent and often down to the metal, which was then rusted over. Not bleeding, but very visible regardless.

Stage One - per my usual process, a primer layer applied via *Mr. Surfacer 1200*.

Rust layer - in anticipation of the volume of rust chips that were going to be visible, I sprayed the entire model in the rust colors.

Faded Russian green layer - admittedly a lot of fun to work with this color scheme, I've always wanted to do one of these heavily faded and chipped subjects for a while. I made my color from simple online photo observations, nothing too fancy, just the right amount of yellow and green together.

The entire model is sprayed with two even layers of hairspray, ready for the green.

I sprayed various darker spots of green to create soft mottled areas seen in photos.

HAIRSPRAY TECHNIQUE

With the outline of the painting set forth, my reference on hand, I started off with a layer of rust over the entire model. Normally, I would spray only the areas I felt I would chip later, but here I knew so many areas were going to be chipped, it was smarter and easier to simply spray the entire model with rust paint. Different to the D9, where I utilized the *Lifecolor Rust* paints because the exposed areas were larger and more visible, here on the T-62M1 I made use of a simpler rust tone, knowing I would later come back and enhance the exposed chips as necessary.

I follow the rust layer with the hairspray, and like I do every time, I sprayed two even layers on, letting it dry in between and completely dry after. The next step was a lot of fun too, I'm very fond of that yellowish green tone to the heavily faded Russian Protective Green No. 2 color and I made my own mixture from *Tamiya* paints, which I then sprayed the entire model with. After the first layer, I added dark green to the paint to adjust the color and sprayed on some random dark spots seen in the reference photos, likely from touch ups over the tank's life.

Now the real fun began. In fact, this is actually the first time I am going to really go all out with the chipping over an entire model. Most extreme subject chipping, even whitewashes are usually in isolated sections for a very specific purpose, and here because of the years of expo-

tips for spraying *Tamiya* paints with water:

• this question has come up a few times in recent discussions since I made the process known that I often thin *Tamiya* acrylics with water when I am going to do some heavy chipping. Here are a few tips that will help with some common issues.

• the thinning ratio is basically the same as I normally do, approx. 50-50 and then mixed thoroughly. If it is too thin, I add more paint, or vice versa. I do not mix with precision, a lot of my paint mixing is by feel and instinct, so this is only a guide.

• to avoid issues, do not spray too wet or too close to the model to avoid cracking in the paint. If this happens, pull the AB back an inch or so and lower your compressor's pressure a few psi.

• the real trick is to spray in very thin light coats from a distance that will dry fast and not leave a pebbly surface. Build the color up slowly, there is no hurry and it is always better to have a superior finish than one that is rushed. Because they are matte paints they will be rougher anyway, however, once we start to scrub the paint with the brush during the chipping process you will see that this action also polishes the paint to a certain degree and this adds to the unique quality of the HS chipping.

PRO-TIP: You can never have too small of a chip, less is more!

thoughts on achieving success with the HS technique and extreme paint chipping:

• arriving at a balanced and natural looking chipping for a subject like this requires practice and experience. I would not recommend starting off with a project like this for your first HS chipping episode. How you hold the brush, how much water is on the surface, how much HS in under the paint and how opaque the top layer is are key factors in the success of this method. You must be honest to the subject too, extreme for the sake of extreme will appear fake and unrealistic, so concentrate on starting off slowly. Try to achieve small very refined chips and scratches first, then expand certain areas to show greater paint wear. It is always a big risk of making mistakes to start with the large chips first.

T-62M1 MAIN BATTLE TANK

The third layer of paint over HS was the camo colors, sprayed to look like they were quickly applied in the field.

thoughts on sealing with a varnish between layers of HS and paint:

• another common question I get asked in regards to the HS technique is whether I spray a protective varnish layer in between the HS and the earlier chipping efforts to protect it. The answer is no, I usually do not, unless I absolutely do not want anything else to happen to it.

• with my normal chipping routine I am very careful and methodical in how I work the chips, rarely do I go back over any area that I have already chipped, even if it is within a new layer on top of the previous one. Anything I do is always in control and if the previous chips expand slightly with new layers, it tends to look natural and flows into the surface effects naturally. I have not experienced a process where I chipped one layer, repeated the HS and paint, chipped that layer and ruined the previous efforts, so I tend to skip the varnish altogether.

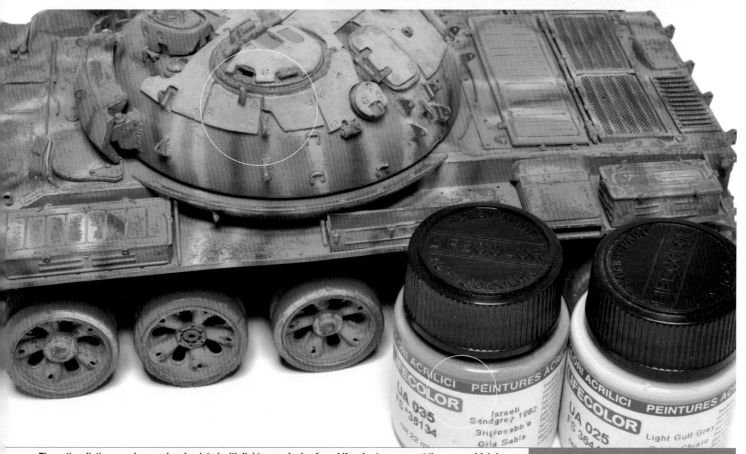

The anti-radiation panels were hand painted with light gray shades from Lifecolor to represent the exposed fabric.

thoughts on painting the radia-tion panels on the turret:

• knowing when to use what tech-nique when and in what order is important to get the right results. It was more efficient to paint and chip all of the painted metal areas of the tank first, then go back and start fresh with the anti-radiation panels. This prevents the tedious task of masking, and because of the simple nature of the panels, it was easier to simply hand paint them afterwards.

• once painting was done I did a quick spot spraying of HS with the AB onto the panels, sprayed the green camo color again (it only required some small patches) and then chipped them to replicate the look of how the paint was severely worn off of the fabric covering on the anti-radiation panels. I then handpainted the fasteners in a dark gray metal color.

Studying the reference photos was so critical to replicating the style of finish, it was a combination of rusting and the paint wear that really was the challenge.

tips on enhancing the darker rust areas :

• when I set about to work with the rust areas, there are many sections of the real tanks that showcased intensely rusted out spots, which were contrasted to some areas where the chipping was very limited. To achieve this look, I worked the HS chipping in line with the ref. photos and once these base chipped areas were established, I then went back over the prominent rust spots with a small piece of sponge and darker rust tones. I carefully "dry-brushed" these rust areas to increase their intensity with the darker tones, which I repeated with even darker colors until I was satisfied with the look.

• this is why it is important to key honed some of the various styles and techniques we have learned over the years. The basic concept of what dry-brushing means is still a very relevant process, and here I used a sponge and dark colors instead of the historical definition of applying lighter tones. Combined with the previous HS chipping, which created the "map" for me to follow I was able to realize the full extent of the paint wear in this manner.

• the anti-radiation panels on top of many Russian tanks are a very unique challenge for us to finish in a convincing manner. Because they are made of a fabric exterior, the look must be realistic to the medium. My efforts to capture that look start by first layering two light gray tones to set the base fabric color, I keep it simple and simply hand paint this step. Then I use some HS followed by the faded green camo and heavy chipping. This process is best to do after the other painting steps, making it a lot easier to facilitate without needing to mask off the panels.

sure and paint wear I could finally go to town with the HS chipping. Needless to say I quite enjoyed myself, and the process worked perfectly. Normal to my routine, I truly kept to the adage of working small sections at a time and constantly referenced my Kabul photos to ensure I was both realistic and *in-scale* with the chipping.

Once the main green color chipping was completed, I could move onto the next range of colors, the hastily applied camo stripes. In this case there were three colors -- light gray, light tan, and black. So back to the HS I went (and like I mentioned before I don't protect with a varnish), which was followed by the three colors being casually airbrushed on, and then chipped in the same manner.

Overall, I spent a long time on this paintjob and its multiple layers of chipping, however it is an extremely efficient process from start to finish and allowed for maximum results and true *in-scale* effects, I had to have success at this stage in order for the model to be considered successful in the end.

Using the sponge dry-brushing technique I describe at the left hand page, I greatly enhanced the layered rust tones on the end of the barrel and bore evacuator.

thoughts on achieving visual balance with extreme painting: ●

• subjects of this nature can and are very attractive choices to model, but they bring with them a lot of challenges and pitfalls if we are not both conscience and respectful of what it is that we are trying to achieve. It would be extremely easy to get carried away and go overboard with the painting on such an extremely chipped and weathered paintjob. How do we keep ourselves in check?

• two main areas are critical; one, is to have the right reference at hand, this helps to both check your work against for accuracy, and to ensure believability. We have the ability to sniff out a fake paintjob, even one so crazy as this one. So check the available sources for your project. Use the internet, both the forums and *Google*, they are tremendous resources.

• two, is the mastery of the techniques used to recreate these effects. You cannot jump feet first into a paintjob of this caliber without first having tested and practiced the techniques -- at the very least! Experience helps. Artists call it *mileage*, and it's best to get very familiar with your tools.

ANTI-RADIATION PANELS

With the tank's paintjob completed, I had to attend to the next step before I could move on to the more extreme layered rust areas. The anti-radiation panels common to modern Soviet armor are fabric covered lead lined panels made of a sandwich style of layers designed to be flexible to drape over the contours of the turret. For this subject, the desert climate had nearly stripped all the paint from the outer layers and again the HS technique really showed its worth by being perfectly capable of replicating this unique effect. All I had to do was note the visual differences and then adjust my quantities of HS and paint to achieve the right look.

In this case, I wanted the HS sprayed only on the panels, so I decanted some into my airbrush and sprayed them directly with one even layer. I then cleaned my AB and filled it with the faded green paint, which I carefully sprayed in very patchy spots on top of the panels, leaving a lot of the gray area exposed. I only did one HS layer because I knew it would not take much effort to chip off so little green paint. And this comes from my years of experience using HS and knowing some of the more subtle effects that can be achieved by manipulating the paint and HS ratios.

A conscious effort was made to illustrate the manner in which the add on parts were much more heavily chipped than the areas painted at the factory.

tips on layering the various chipped area effects to achieve a successful result:

• this paintjob hinged on my ability to effectively layer the multiple special effects in such a manner that I achieved all my requirements of accuracy and in-scale realism. This required some forethought to properly plan my way towards this end results, and I started with how best to showcase the exposed rust tones. Once resolved, I then planned the camo chipping followed by the anti-radiation panel painting, and lastly the turret numbers, (which are the only markings on the model). Each step was accomplished via the hairspray technique and I controlled my results by altering the quantity and opacity of each product to create the variety of chipped areas. The dark rust patches were then specifically attended to by applying the darkest rust tones on each individual chipped mark both via small sponges and via handpainting.

RUST TONES

To reinforce my earlier comments in the chapter on OPR in the beginning of the book, you will notice a very distinct visual change in the rust areas from the time the model was chipped and after the anti-radiation panels were painted. The myriad of rust areas were also enhanced to realize their full potential. To achieve this I chose to paths to get to the end result. The first was to actually hand paint in some of the darker tones using both a #2 round paint brush and dark rust colors, and small pieces of sponge where appropriate to create a stippled rusted effect, as seen on the end of the main gun barrel.

The point to make with this effort is that the process of enhancing the rust chips was very simple and straightforward. Why? Because the process of how the model is chipped during the HS technique ultimately becomes a *road map* for me to follow, and all I had to do was keep my references handy to ensure that I had I created balanced visual effects. It really was that fundamental and basic. I've started to follow this path with the weathered effects, where the initial painting and chipping now direct what is to follow next. The result is a much more relaxed and enjoyable experience and the stress is lowered because we are not forcing the artificial randomness into the model, it happens in a much more natural fashion this way.

OPR was used to render the various darker worn metal areas, enhance the rust tones and begin the dust layers.

thoughts on evaluating the results at the major steps to ensure a successful result:

• I discuss this thought process a few times in the previous **TANKART** volumes with the intent to get you to become a better judge of where your work is headed. A lot of what scale modeling is about is the correlation between the historical vehicle and our interpretation of them in a scale environment. Stopping to review the work in-progress at key moments is an effective way to keep ourselves going down the right path. Are my effects realistic? Does it look interesting? How accurate are my colors? The list of questions can go on and on...what becomes of this is that we begin to feel the way the model is going; the vibe we are getting from it is important. I think this is one area why so many models end up as shelf queens before they see the finish line. Wrong turns are taken and then we get stuck, and part of my doing these books is to help the greater collective push through these difficult situations when they do arise. It becomes an asset to be able to adjust your workflow, techniques, and the products we use to guide the outcome to where we had always hoped the project would land. No project is ever perfect, and that is frankly part of the hobby's charm, but we can gain confidence and efficiency to complete the projects we start by being more in control of how the finish is going to look on each model. It won't happen right away, and like all the other things we do in modeling, repetition and experience quickly become our friends.

thoughts on working with heavily worn finishes and the oils:

• it's hard for me to completely contain my enthusiasm for working on such a project, the efforts were a lot of fun and what really helps is taking the finish to the next level. Working with oils is such a rewarding experience and here I was able to fully exploit such a finite amount that had huge results. When I started to work the oils into the paint, I was able to finally bring out the various tones and developed a rhythm of adjusting the darker rust areas alongside the light faded dust tones. The brush work also begins a subtle polishing effect that imparts a nice sheen and this works towards presenting this as painted metal. Again the power of oil paints seems to endless in our world and I strongly recommend their use. Being able to control each brush stroke and achieve the desired results is fast becoming a staple of my weathering, this model really brought that home for me.

I kept the oil colors relevant to the tones already on the model, which is a crucial yet subtle element to giving the model that desolate appearance.

• the comments I make on page 80 are at work in the image to the left. I felt something was missing, even though I was really enjoying where the finish was going. It was a bit too even, as it related to the photos. Almost monochromatic in fact, the model still needed something more. Often we turn to figures and stowage in such cases, but I had to rely on less to create more. However, the solution was already present, I just had to see it! In related Kabul photos I had noticed many vehicles had been spot sprayed in a garish bright dark green in many areas and this color didn't correlate to any other camo scheme, but it was clearly used. Thus, I picked out the top hatch and a few road wheels with a heavily chipped rendition of this color.

Continuing with the HS efforts, I spot sprayed some areas in a bright dark green and heavily chipped it off, as seen in many Kabul vehicle photos.

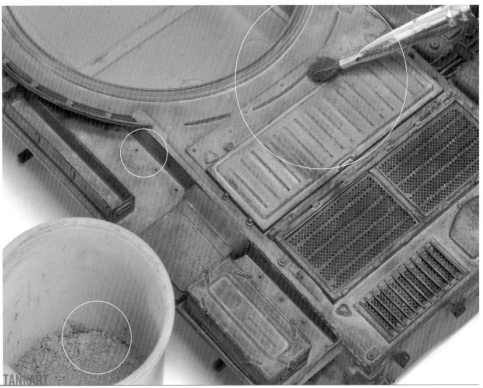

PIGMENTS

From here the model has progressed to a very advanced weathering stage with two major principles in play, the HS technique painting/chipping efforts, followed by the OPR weathering. The final third element to apply was the pigments, and in this particular case, (in stark contrast to the D9R project), the pigments were used in an extremely limited application to represent just a minimal amount of accumulated dust on the model. Kabul reference photos showed these abandoned vehicles and tanks only had a small amount of dust present, most likely a result of the desert winds constantly blowing them relatively clean. So I applied the dust pigments in the very traditional sense of using a small brush and rubbing them in only a few select places along the exposed fenders and top hull. To complete the process, I used a quick pass with the fixer sprayed from my airbrush to set them in place.

The use of pigments was extremely limited here, only using small amounts to represent some dust.

The model is nearing the finish line, so the bulk of my last weathering efforts turns toward finalizing the small details and ensuring the resulting elements are convincing and ultimately balanced overall.

thoughts and tips on painting tracks, and how they compare to my previous models: ●

• on this model I went with kit tracks and used a color setup unlike any I've painted before. Usually, they get replaced with *Friulmodel* sets, and I take the track colors along the rather typical path of dark metal and heavy rust tones (using *Blacken-it*) and loaded with earthen effects. But here I had the unique opportunity to go a different route, and the quality of the kit tracks was suitable enough and easy to work with. Photos showed these to have lighter tones resulting from the lack of being driven on for years, so I started by painting them a pale gray color with soft rust overtones, followed by darker rust washes. I finished them on the model with darker rust tones using sponges and dark rust paint.

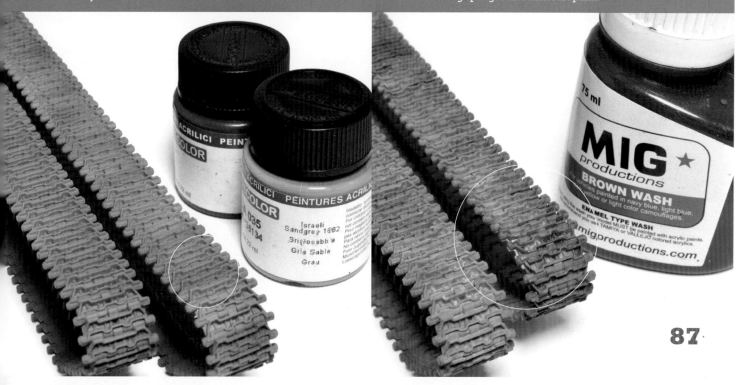

87

THE FINAL DETAILS

The pigments went rather quickly in all honesty, with so little required I was able to complete that step in no time. That left only a few more areas to attend to realize the project's goals. One was to add a bit more color to the model via another fast round of HS and chipped paint. On the commander's hatch and two road wheels on the left side, I applied a layer of dark bright green, which was heavily chipped according to some additional reference photos I had seen online. I also took some white *Humbrol* enamel paint and handpainted a lot number on the front hull, again using the Kabul pictures to guide me, which also places this tank in the correct time frame of after the Allies have secured the facility and done a "head count" of the vehicles present.

All that was left to complete the model, was to mount the tracks and finish them off. With the tank immobile for years, the tracks had taken on a pale tan-gray color with lots of old rust on the surface, with no brightly worn areas or heavy earth effects. This was easy to replicate after I had base painted them. I used a small sponge and darker rust paint with a stippling and dry-brushing technique to finish the project.

thoughts on the comparative argument of less equals more applied to this project: ●

• this model was very unique in how it played into the greater scheme of replicating historical subjects. It's probably fair to say that most of the projects we work on are of the active variety, meaning set in combat or peacetime settings as functioning tanks. Here we have an abandoned tank and this takes on a different set of painting challenges. While I can't state for certain which led to what being developed first, but the use of oil paints to take over from the more traditional filter and pinwash stages into this arena where I went straight from the paintjob into using the oils to realize the weathering is a key element in the scheme of how this model came about. I was able to use less product and techniques and come up with a very convincing result in the end. This being another set of tools for us to use going forward.

The empty fenders and open storage box were easy mods to make this model a convincing abandoned tank. The dark green wheels add a splash more color.

thoughts on utilizing key areas to increase visual interest:

• with a model like this, you would think the extreme paintjob alone would be sufficient visual stimuli, but once I got to a certain point in the finish it still needed some more to take it to that "just right" level. I used small elements on the model itself to capture this effect: the open hub, the chipped turret numbers, the handpainted lot number on the nose, and the multiple spots on dark bright green all work together to add another layer of visual interest to the final look without even adding figures or stowed material yet, which would most likely be the next logical step to further set it off.

thoughts on the *Trumpeter* and *MIG Productions* conversion set: ●

• we are indeed very lucky to be in this position where we now have a lot of new modern releases, in fact by the time you read this 2013 will have been a banner year of new Russian kits, especially from *Trumpeter*. *MIG productions* were keen to grab some headlines with this conversion and it proved very popular. The first batch issues being undersized aside, the turret is an excellent representation of the subject and I felt it was the perfect canvas for the painting efforts. In fact, it was hard to decide on which Kabul subject to paint, there being a few that had a lot of good reference photos for. In the end I wanted to depict the heavy rust and worn paint, and I've always wanted to paint a Russian tank in the heavily faded green that is almost yellow green in color. Overall, one of the best projects I had the pleasure to work on.

T-62M1 Main Battle Tank   ●

In the greater scheme of where I am headed with my work, this project was a pivotal model that provided a solid foundation in a few key areas of painting and weathering. By this time, I have had a lot of experience using the HS technique for chipping paint and now I had the chance to expand upon my thoughts about combining the OPR concept I discussed earlier to completely take over the weathering before I get into using the pigments. The specific challenges of this project were the right combination of elements to take this concept to its full implementation, and that success was fruitful for both myself as a modeler and for the boxart itself with an accurate depiction of the subject.

What I find exciting for the future is that overall I was happy with how it went and why it worked so well. That level of confirmation is how I gain confidence for the next model and that can't be underestimated. While I won't switch to this process for every single project I make, I do like the fact I will have the opportunity to integrate the ideas learned into certain models when the process fits right within the overall goal of the project. And this goes beyond armor as well. There are a lot of other related subjects that this combination of HS painting/chipping and the OPR weathering to gain the best from it will work well with. But I don't want to spoil anything, I still have a lot of armor models to complete before I get the chance to try my hand with other genres.

RUSSIAN MBT T-62M1 (Afghan)

1/35 Trumpeter T-62 mod.1972, MIG Prod. T-62M1 conversion

RUSSIAN MBT T-62M1 (Afghan)

1 PRIMER

RUSTED METAL BASE

HS LAYER #1

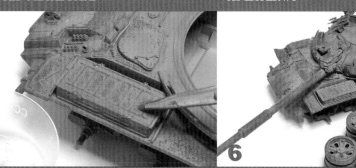

4 FADED GREEN CAMO

HS CHIPPING #1

6 HS CHIPPING #1

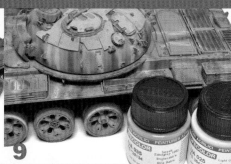

7 CAMO COLORS OVER HS #2

8 HS CHIPPING #2

9 ANTI-RADIATION PANELS PAINTED

10 TURRET RUST

11 MAIN GUN RUST

12 TURRET NUMBERS OVER HS#3

QUICK REF SBS

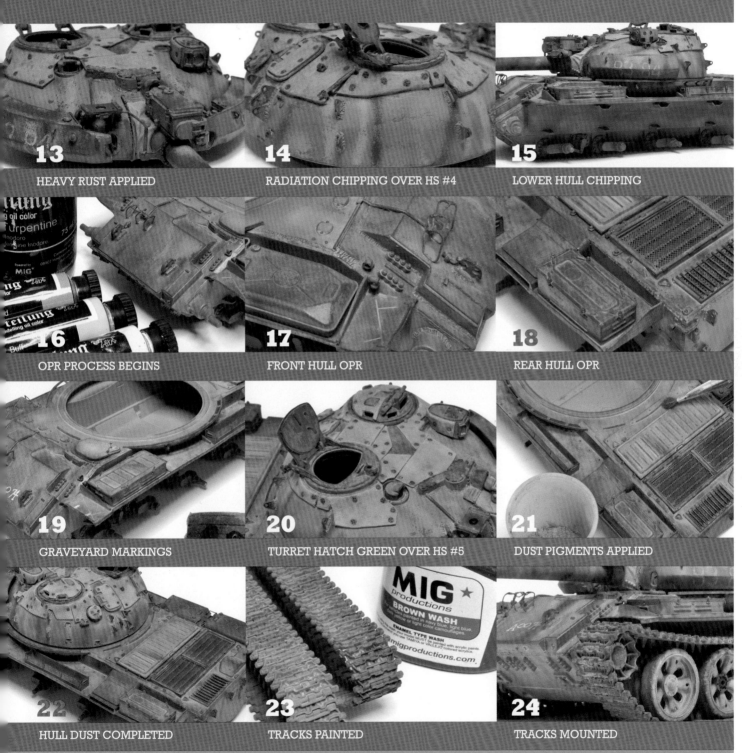

13 HEAVY RUST APPLIED

14 RADIATION CHIPPING OVER HS #4

15 LOWER HULL CHIPPING

16 OPR PROCESS BEGINS

17 FRONT HULL OPR

18 REAR HULL OPR

19 GRAVEYARD MARKINGS

20 TURRET HATCH GREEN OVER HS #5

21 DUST PIGMENTS APPLIED

22 HULL DUST COMPLETED

23 TRACKS PAINTED

24 TRACKS MOUNTED

FRENCH MBT AMX-30B

1/35 MENG French Army MBT AMX-30B

French MBT AMX-30B

I was particularly excited when new manufacturer *MENG Models* arrived on the modeling scene. Within a very short period of time an entirely new kit maker appeared and began the onslaught of some amazing releases that covered so many vibrant areas lacking with other current releases.

Immediate post-war Western armor design is such an untapped market I immediately jumped at the chance to build the latest *MENG* kit -- 1/35 French AMX-30B, and while there has always been the *Heller* kits, they are quite old and long in the tooth lacking the modern fit and finish we are so spoiled with today. As it is, I'm a fan of the look of this rather sleek design and the advent of *Friulmodel* adding a new metal track set specific to this vehicle, I had all I needed to convince myself to include this model within these pages.

One thing I strive for with each title is to cover a wide variety of schemes regarding the subjects and here I had a good opportunity to portray the 3-tone NATO camouflage scheme, however I planned a slight twist to it. The kit itself makes the earlier versions and these have now been relegated to range or guard duty posts, which means some substantial paint wear is in play. Thankfully today we have the internet as a viable photo resource and I discovered a site specific to this variant and many amazing photos of old veteran AMX-30Bs left abandoned on the various army ranges. The size and shape closely proximate Russian armor of the time period, so they were the perfect OPFOR tank of choice, and those were now left to have fate decide how best to discard them.

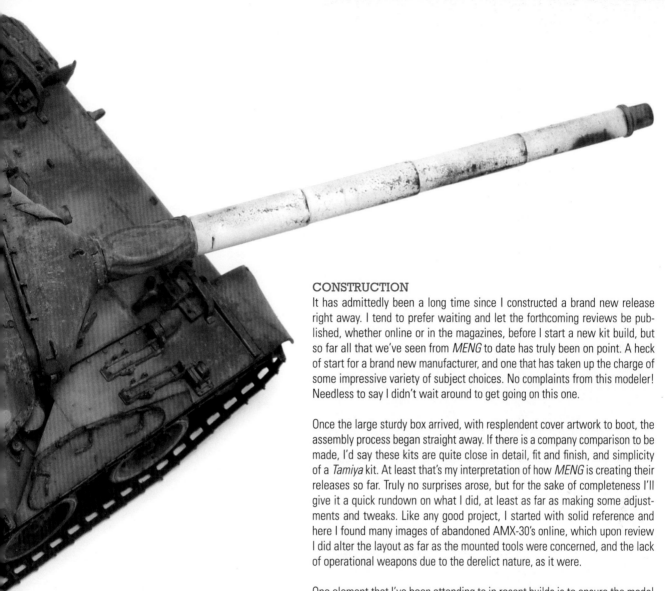

CONSTRUCTION

It has admittedly been a long time since I constructed a brand new release right away. I tend to prefer waiting and let the forthcoming reviews be published, whether online or in the magazines, before I start a new kit build, but so far all that we've seen from *MENG* to date has truly been on point. A heck of start for a brand new manufacturer, and one that has taken up the charge of some impressive variety of subject choices. No complaints from this modeler! Needless to say I didn't wait around to get going on this one.

Once the large sturdy box arrived, with resplendent cover artwork to boot, the assembly process began straight away. If there is a company comparison to be made, I'd say these kits are quite close in detail, fit and finish, and simplicity of a *Tamiya* kit. At least that's my interpretation of how *MENG* is creating their releases so far. Truly no surprises arose, but for the sake of completeness I'll give it a quick rundown on what I did, at least as far as making some adjustments and tweaks. Like any good project, I started with solid reference and here I found many images of abandoned AMX-30's online, which upon review I did alter the layout as far as the mounted tools were concerned, and the lack of operational weapons due to the derelict nature, as it were.

One element that I've been attending to in recent builds is to ensure the model sits squat and looks heavy, like a true to scale piece of armor. It's a subtle thing, something that would likely go unnoticed, and from observations in general, I am trying to impart a subtle suspension settling and lend the model some visual weight. To do this, especially here on the AMX with its adjustable suspension setup, I add lead weight inside the lower hull during the gluing process and let the lower hull and mounted suspension arms set up overnight under this weight (the weight sits in there loose). What this does is settle the model down a millimeter or so, and gives a more squat stance. Like I said it's really a visual fine-tuning, you may not even see it at first glance, but trust me it's there.

thoughts on the things that make us strive for creating a truly original project: ●

• this project was unique in a couple of ways; one being the subject itself, a somewhat obscure (by today's standards) post-war French tank, but one that played a key role in French armor theories and designs. I like that sort of historical significance. The other being it's a brand new kit from a brand new manufacturer, so there is a bit to celebrate in the fact the hobby is still a very healthy enterprise, and *MENG* have fielded an impressive array of new kits in both the armor and aircraft markets. I try to source motivation where ever it may lie, and this fact alone makes me feel energized to truly do this model justice with the paintjob.

With the lower hull assembled to my satisfaction, the rest of the hull is built per the instructions, followed by the turret in typical armor modeling construction sequences. Two areas I usually attend to with each kit build is to thin plastic fenders and drill out any tubular opening for weapons, or the like. Thinning plastic parts still plays a vital role in my modeling and it's a good skill to keep honed.

That said, I also wasn't happy with the extremely smooth turret casting itself, and decided to add a very subtle level of cast texture to the turret. Now, this is tricky because photos do show it relatively smooth in general, but given the plan for the paintjob coming afterwards some texture was going to be very useful later. I will need some grit to the surface in other words, but more on that when I get to the painting sections. I also used the time to add two prominent weld beads missing along the top of the hull edges, laying styrene strips in the joint, applying glue to soften them so I can add some texture.

From here I can now focus on the smaller details. Because my subject is an abandoned one, the exterior fittings for the tools and the secondary weapons were all removed, and since the kit tools are typical all-in-one affairs, I had to find an alternative method to show them. Fortunately, post-war tool clamps for both French and German armor are essentially carry over items from German WWII clamp designs, at least for the purposes of this small scale. So I simply used an *Aber* WWII German PE set as my primary detailing agent for the empty tool clamps. However, to fit them properly I had to first fill the original part's mounting holes, and add the other basic fittings from styrene to illustrate them accurately. Again, like all mods, I used some good reference photos to create a close approximation of the look I was going for.

The rear hull area is cleaned up and all new tool fittings are added with PE and styrene.

The original kit parts provides nice details for the rear telephone box.

thoughts on the various track options:

• one element to the older *Heller* kits that was loathed by most modelers were the horrible stiff plastic vinyl one-piece tracks. They truly sucked. Thankfully, *MENG* paid close attention and provides us with superb link-to-link plastic ones in the box, so that takes care of that issue. However, *Friulmodel* also has released two metal track sets for the AMX-30 series (both the original chevron design used here, and the later square rubber block Diehl style too), and naturally I couldn't resist the temptation to use them for this project. In large part because the reference photos showed a style of rust to the old tracks on those particular tanks and I knew using Blacken-it solution would be the ultimate process to capture the look properly.

• I also noticed with these tanks, old or not, the tracks are very taut and have nearly no sag, so by switching to Friuls I would actually have an easier time getting the right tension look from them.

thoughts on adding the subtle cast surface texture for the turret:

• I mention in the text that I added some cast texture via brushing on *Gunze Mr. Surfacer 1000* and stippling it as dried. But the trick to this to then sand the texture after it dries, which is what gives us the low areas and pits to the metal. The real cast turrets are quite smooth and I had to be careful not to overdo the effect, but the chipped paint planned later would be a lot easier to pull off with some texture to work with.

FRENCH MBT AMX-30B

paint callouts for the AMX-30B project:

NATO 3-TONE (chipped)

• **1st layer - RUST UNDERCOAT**: Due to the nature of the multi-layered chipping process, the first color applied is a rust tone.

• **2nd layer - French Army OD**: This is the starting off color using a mix of *Lifecolor UA 224 Olive Drab Faded 2* and *UA 437 Deep IDF Green*.

• **2nd layer - NATO GREEN**: This is the first NATO color using *Tamiya XF-67 NATO Green*.

• **3rd layer - NATO BROWN**: The next camo color applied is *Tamiya XF-68 NATO Brown*.

• **4th layer - NATO BLACK**: The final camo color applied is *Tamiya XF-69 NATO Black*. All of these colors are applied over a layer of HS.

quick ref:
• RUST BASE: Lifecolor Rust set

• French OD: UA 224 Olive Drab UA 437 Dp IDF Grn

• NATO Green: XF-67 NATO Green

• NATO Brown: XF-68 NATO Brown

• NATO Black: XF-69 NATO Black

PAINTING BEGINS

Time to get serious with this project. The intensity of what is about to happen cannot be underscored enough to emphasize the importance of both research and balance with the multiple layered colors that are going to receive some heavy wear and tear. A proper primer coat is essential and I decided to use the new acrylic airbrush primer from *AK Interactive* this time. That being said, the one real advantage to using an acrylic primer is that I can spray it indoors without resorting to going outside for using my trusty *Mr. Surfacer*. That's helpful in the winter and when you live in community apartments making it difficult to find a quiet spot to spray primer, (which is both new to me). Such is the life of scale modeler!

The AMX-30's also had a rather unique scheme in that the entire lower areas are solid black, which allowed me to utilize two primer colors and give the model a head start on the color scheme at the same time. I sprayed the model in the *Grey* primer first followed with the *Black* primer down low and underneath. Overall, I found the

thoughts on the new acrylic style primers :

• one of things I set out to do with these books is to not represent just one brand, or one line of products. I decided early on I want to work alongside like-minded manufacturers to co-develop and utilize dedicated hobby products whenever possible. I start my association with the newly reorganized *AK Interactive* as a result of this effort. These new acrylic primers are a newer product and further the ends of being able to work solely indoors, so on that level I recommend their use. While I'm not a fan of going to the airbrush for anything except painting, I was happy the primers sprayed and cleaned up easily enough, something that's hard to do with Mr. Surfacer in the jars. Of course, I'll always love and use the aerosol primers, but these are indeed worthy substitute options.

Stage One - the model is primed in both grey and black, the later as a camo color

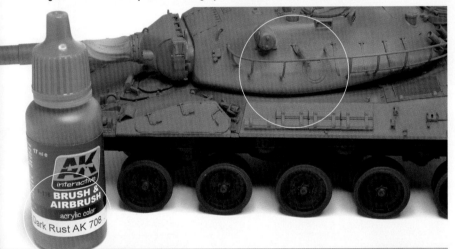

Stage Two - the underlying rust layer is applied, which represents chipped paint to the metal.

Stage Three - the model is given two even layers of HS to prep it for the next round of painting.

new primers worked good. Perhaps a bit more tedious a process since it involves the airbrush and the associated cleaning, but the lack of strong odors and general ease of use and quality adhesion were noticeable.

From here I immediately jumped into the first color application. To reiterate, this model is intentionally going to see some extreme paint wear and flaking because the subject was placed outdoors on ranges for years and were exposed to the four seasons and the many elements of being a non-service tank. A fantastic reference website to see these (and most other French armor) vehicles in their neglected states is http://www.chars-francais.net and search under *1966 AMX-30B*, there are a lot of excellent images of them, including close-ups showing the extreme paint wear, rust and heavy chipping. So given that, next up is the underlying rust tones. This will facilitate the final chipping later on and give me that true depth to the paint chips I desperately seek with such HS chipping efforts.

HAIRSPRAY CHIPPING - ROUND 1

By now the prep and application process for using HS as a chipping medium is becoming a fairly routine process. I typically write up the text after I'm a few steps further along and I can say the results from this were about as close to what I see in the references for layered weathered chips that I've yet been able to achieve. So I write this part of the chapter with a big smile on my face! I love it when a plan comes together, and here my experience is

The original 1960's French OD faded green camo is applied next, mixed from *Lifecolor UA224 & UA 437*.

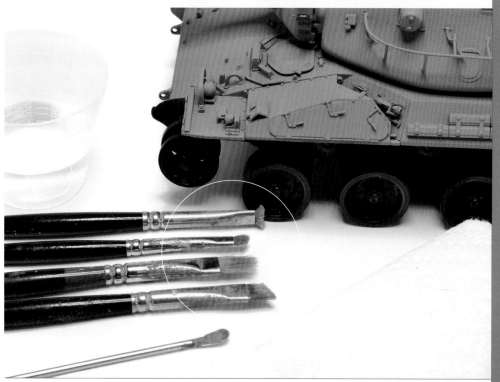

The tools used for proper and efficient HS chipping. The paper towel is essential as well.

tips on the HS chipping:

• the HS chipping on this particular subject is quite a bit different in its final outcome to those in the previous chapters, namely because here the paint has to illustrate the flaky style associated with old neglected subjects. The surface is outdoors 100% of the time and the effects of sun, exposure and moisture all work against it to create a cracked and flaky chipped appearance that cuts through the many layers of paint applied in the tank's service life.

• because of this initial need I decided to work *Lifecolor* acrylics since the tend to have that exact chipping characteristic -- flaky.

• the other aspect of the process is that I change my hand's movement and the type of brush I use, working instead with more stabbing motions and a brush with splayed out bristles that can sort of pick and pry the paint up versus my more common motion of using the edge of the bristles in a side-to-side type of movement.

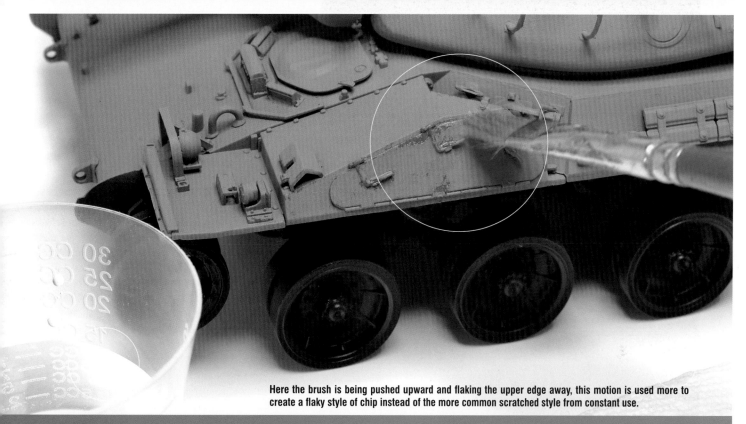

Here the brush is being pushed upward and flaking the upper edge away, this motion is used more to create a flaky style of chip instead of the more common scratched style from constant use.

thoughts on the ability of HS chipping to be controlled to give us the type of chips specifically desired:

• HS paint chipping is a powerful tool and learning how to work with its strengths is going to see it give you incredible results. The two elements at work on how we control this function and get the type of chip we are after are: 1) the amount of water applied to the surface, and how long you let it sit, 2) the brush type and the bristles, and 3) your hand movement and the motion of how you attack the surface. Again all things take time to learn and practice, but I switch from side-to-side motions and run the edge of the brush along the edge of the model's surface and this creates fine scratch like chips, but by stabbing and lifting you can achieve a larger flake type of chip seen here.

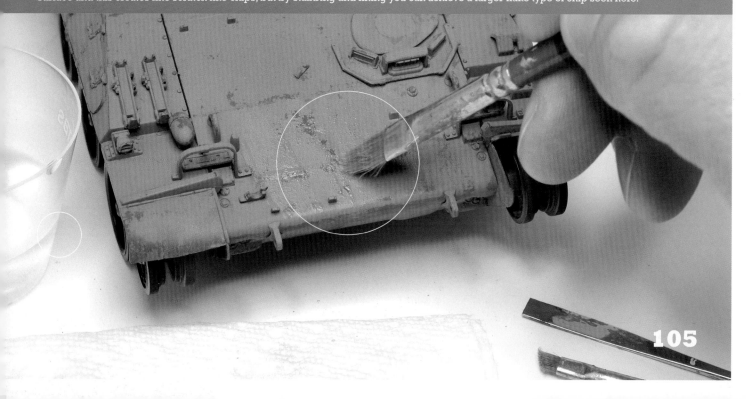

thoughts on evaluating this project's painting goals: ●

• when I typically sit down to start a new project I like to consider a few factors that will weigh heavily on the direction the model takes. With a tank like the AMX-30, it arguably is a rather boring subject choice and in and of itself does not drum up that much excitement. I get that. While I've liked it since I first saw one, I know it lacks that certain "wow" factor. So with that in mind, it takes some effort to source a good point of reference to instill a lot of what is missing from that element. In that vein, I was lucky in that many of these saw out the end of their service lives out sitting on French armor ranges and that allowed the main element I am most concerned with, the paintjob, to become something far more interesting and visually more appealing. Plus, painting it up will be both a challenge and more fun.

• the other important element at work is the fact I can process a true NATO scheme for the first time, and that will have a far reaching influence for so many other modern armor subjects we have new kits for like the Leopard, M1's, M109's, and other vehicles of this era. So this model does carry weight for illustrating that type of 3-tone scheme, which is another aspect to **TANKART** and the intent to cover a wide variety of patterns used around the world.

showing and that is something I truly want to convey to you, the reader. So much of the success generated with modeling will come essentially from time and patience -- and a whole lot of practice. That should really be the most important element you take away from these books, if there is just one concept at the core, it is really that.

So to properly apply the HS, I hold the model at arm's length (in my left hand, since I'm a righty), and spray the HS from just before the model until just after with each pass that is brisk and linear in movement, and from a distance of approx. 12" away (approx. 25cm for my metric clients). You can see the sheen lay down and it should look even and semi-glossy. Not super wet looking, but have a strong glossy perception to it. After I cover the model with HS (I spray the hull and turret separately), I dry with a hairdryer until the surface is dry to the touch. Then I repeat with a slightly lesser amount for the second layer, which is then also dried off. This has become my standard application process for HS, and more times than not, the results are very controllable and success can be achieved.

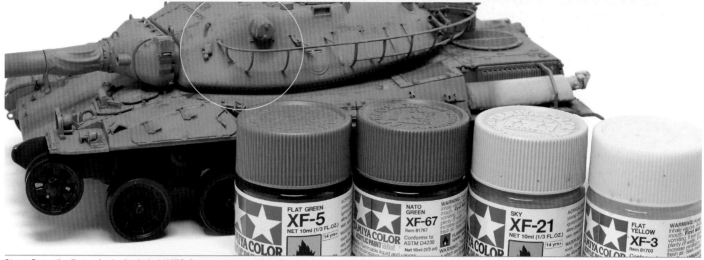

Stage One - the first color is the faded NATO Green - approx. 40% *XF-5 Ft. Green*, 40% *XF-67 NATO Green*, and 10% each of *XF-21 Sky* and *XF-3 Ft. Yellow*.

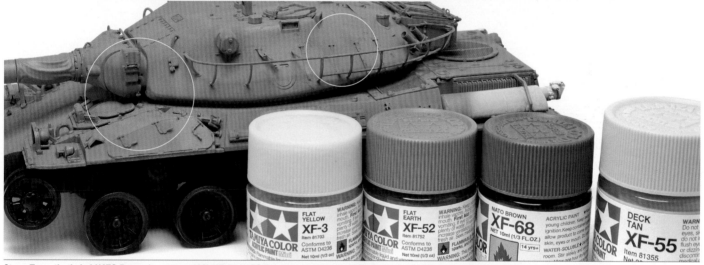

Stage Two - the faded NATO Brown is approx. 40% *XF-68 NATO Brown* and 40% *XF-52 Ft. Earth*, and 10% each of *XF-3 Ft. Yellow* and *XF-55 Deck Tan*.

Stage Three - the faded NATO Black is made up of approx. 80% *XF-69 NATO Black*, and 10% each of *XF-12 J.N. Grey* and *XF-23 Light Blue*.

Working with a triple layered chipping process at work, I am careful to keep my movements extremely controlled and focused on each area.

tips on working in small sections:

• the paint wear on this model is very different to the other projects I've attempted, and the best method to employ is to go slowly, patiently and work in very small sections and create the exact look you're after. Here I want the top NATO paint colors to flake off to show the faded OD green underneath, and then the next layer of chips the show the rusted metal.

• part of the reason for the chipping success is that the NATO colors are each applied very thinly and this allows far finer control and the chips happen easier and with greater precision. By working with the airbrushing to utilize the advantages I've created to this point the chips become more effective, and the look of the worn out paintjob is much more realistic and effective looking.

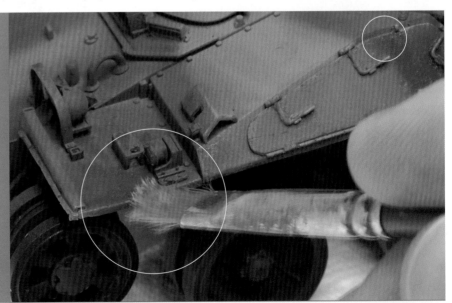

The style of chips has to reflect the service life of the subject and I create subtle variations between those marks caused by something hitting the surface vs. those flaking off type of chip from old age.

Reference photos are carefully studied to evaluate the paint's surface effects and I work each section to take advantage of this level of detail in the chipping.

tips for using the chipping effects to illustrate different stories and materials:

• this model has some unique aspects that if properly utilized create a very different look than many other projects. For example, the exhaust have a high alloy content and they don't rust out like steel exhausts, some very distinct reference photos show this and I thought it a great idea to incorporate into the finished scheme. The paint wear was vastly different in intensity due to the high heat exposure the original paint had to endure. The spare tracks (above), were another interesting area and this is just the first level of chipping and rusting for them. Because the spare tracks were never primed, the paint sticks far less and we can create another unique focal point on this model. Overall, the type of chips, how many layers I'm going through are all implemented to work as a whole and tell story of this tank's long life.

thoughts on setting the stage:

• over the course of a project you'll reach a sort of midway point in the finish and things will happen largely along the path you've now created, that road-map for the weathering is largely in place now. It's pretty difficult to alter the finish along another direction, so it plays a hand in how the final model will turn out. Obviously, on this AMX-30B, I am committed to the presentation of a worn out and end-of-service MBT, so now I will begin to exceute the second phase of the plan and concentrate on the weathering aspects.

• traditionally we see filters, washes, oils, and pigments as the tools of the trade. On this project I'm going to start to use a bunch of new products that have hit the market in recent months from a few different companies like *Lifecolor, Vallejo, Wilder,* and *AK Interactive*. I'm excited to see the results. It's a cool spot to be in as I write this chapter, the hobby is in the amazing state of change and here we have a new kit, and a host of new products to work with. Sure we don't always need them, but part of it is to support and create a culture of innovation too.

thoughts for constantly using the Hairspray chipping technique: ●

• I obviously spend a large amount of space and time talking about HS chipping. It's important to continually go over and discuss this technique because even though I'm illustrating a vast array of paint wear and tear, the power of HS (like OPR) is that you have a lot of control on the quantity at work. It doesn't always have to look this extreme, but the realistic level of worn paint is hard to ignore. Looking at the images above and below, to achieve this and have the chips on the correct layers and provide a 3D effect all on its own is a truly remarkable stage of the game for us. Thus I feel obligated to expand on every aspect of this powerful tool as much as I possibly can.

• on a side note for the turret that I treated with Mr. Surfacer in the construction phase, well it paid of by allowing just enough texture to create these flaky chips perfectly.

The results of the mutliple layers of HS chipping through the NATO camo and green base coat.

What follows next is the first layer of paint, the faded French OD Green from the 1960's. This color starts off as a deep dark green but quickly fades to a much lighter shade, and I mixed up a batch from *Lifecolor UA 224 Faded OD Type 2* and *UA 437 Deep IDF Green* from their new Camouflage Series of paint sets. This are thinned with water and airbrushed lightly over the model. A very straightforward step, I then proceed to create the array of flaked paint chips and some smaller scratched ones too. After, I immediately go into applying another full round of HS in preparation for the NATO Camo scheme. Here you have a choice, you can spray the model with a flat varnish at this point to seal it up so no more chips occur to the green. I actually did because the sheer volume of chipping involved. But it's not a hard rule for me. Your choice really.

HAIRSPRAY CHIPPING - ROUND 2
Now comes the main application of the NATO colors. However, like the rest of the paint it too is heavily faded. So simply using a NATO paint set straight out of the bottle is not the complete answer for this project. Instead, I use the *Tamiya NATO* paints as the starting off point, and add in a host of lighter tones to create the actual shades that I ultimately spray. If you'll notice coverage is fairly thorough, but I do leave a level of transparency to the scheme because this further enhances the worn out paint effect I'm after. And like all my HS applications, the

thoughts on working with the new *Windex* paint wear technique:

• I love new techniques and for a while now there have been efforts on working out a reliable process to rub off the top layer of paint to show the underlying color. For the sharp chips that are common with armor, the Hairspray technique is obviously a favorite on my bench, but I've worked with thinners as a way to gently rub away the top paint in a much softer manner. I used this idea in **TANKART 1** and **2** with lacquer thinner. But it is potent and doesn't work well when cutting through more than just the one top color.

• enter the work of *Marc Ruesser* and *John Tolcher*, names you may be familiar with it you are active on the internet modeling forums. *Marc* has come up with a system of paint wear that works using *Windex* (an ammonia based window cleaner) diluted with water and *Tamiya* acrylics. The basic premise is to spray the first color and seal it with Dullcote, then spray the other colors you want to cut through followed by the top layer, all thinned with *Lacquer Thinner*. Then take a solution of 1:1 *Windex*-to-water and scrub the paint. The solution wears away the outer layers of paint until the base layer is revealed, which creates a very realistic worn off layered paint effect. *John* has built some amazing projects with it. Arguably, armor models won't use this concept too much because this effect is a process that takes years of exposure to facilitate in real life. But here on this AMX-30B that has been doing exactly that, I used this technique on the white barrel with limited success. Like all good ideas though, practice is the key element and I plan to use it a lot for some future projects.

three separate color mixtures were all thinned with water and to be honest they sprayed beautifully with little to no overspray. The trick is to apply them in very thin coats, the first being a wet coat, which helps to prevent orange peel surface from them drying before they hit the model's surface.

With that task completed, arguably a lot of painting, I could now get into the chipping for the main visual elements. I repeat the process, same as I did with the green base color and work to show a layered chipping effect. To that end, I also attempted another similar chipping process with the main gun barrel. These derelict AMX-30s often had their main gun barrels painted white while on the range (or perhaps for another reason?...), and the wear is slightly different to the look created from HS chipping. As explained at left, I used the newer *Windex* paint wear process to mixed effect. I definitely need more time with it to perfect, but I liked where I was headed with it.

REFINISHING THE WHEELS

At this point I had to turn my attention back to the road wheels for some extra attention. Derelict vehicles have specific elements of wear and tear and I had to process the wheels next before I could start the main bulk of the weath-

The wheels were repainted to show a variety of paint wear between the NATO black and faded OD.

• this project was very unique in that the lower areas were an opportunity to illustrate a totally different visual effect than a regular operational vehicle covered in the usual mud and dirt effects. When scanning the various reference images I could see on the tanks that were parked in the field and left to rot that many had old dried up mud, tire rubber, and a combination of rust and moss had begun to take over. Very cool visual effects! The moist wet climate of France in the countrysides gives me, the author, a really original finishing concept that is unlike the bulk of my models.

• I was also able to utilize some new products as well. For pigments I tried the new line developed by Adam Wilder called *Wilder*. I used them as I always do -- I mixed up a batch of 3-4 colors, applied the mix dry, then added a liquid fixer, in this case *Tamiya X-20A thinner*, to set them in place. I found the results to be excellent, and as good as *MiG Productions* pigments, which are the main ones I've been using. I also used some of the special effect enamels from *AK Interactive*, namely the *Slime Green Light*, *Kursk Earth* and the *Light Rust Wash*. Each gave good results and it was nice to actually use the *Slime Green Light* for once. I don't build dioramas and believe the color is best suited for moss effects commonly seen on old buildings, but here I had that exact requirement and it did the job nicely. One trick was to apply these colors on top of the pigments, because they are near invisible against the black hull paint otherwise.

The wheels were weathered with layers of *Wilder* pigments, exposed rusted metal and stains, plus a dust wash build-up indicative of a stationary vehicle.

The pigment application is my tried-and-true process of setting the model on its side to create a horizontal surface, apply the pigments dry in random patches and then hit it with a liquid fixer to set them in place. Here I'm using *Wilder's* new pigments for the first time I mixed 4 light tones to create the color above.

thoughts on building up the layers of heavy weathering:

• in addition to the thought process I expressed earlier within the CAT D9 Dozer chapter in regards to *layering*, it is important to continue this discussion because this AMX-30B project really required the concept to unfold in the right way and in the right order to be successful in the end. With as much wear and tear to the paint that I'm showing, it's a critical element to handle certain processes at specific times. For example, here I have to get the pigments onto the lower hull surface before I can mount the wheels and tracks for the final time. Once this is done I am completely free to now focus solely on the paint wear representations. While obvious, it's still a good refresher to keep us on track, pun intended, because what comes next is the type of weathering that will truly define the model's finish and create the look that leaves a lasting impression, the success of the model will depend on it. As I said in this chapter's beginning, being able to turn a rather subdued subject into something really memorable will require a deft touch and clear understanding of the power of being able to layer the chipped paint correctly, apply the weathering in the right stages, and finally wrap it all up with the OPR process. All of which work in combination to realize the end result that I had planned out early on.

ering. I start by doing some quick HS chipping with the original green camo, photos showed the wheels have a lot of paint wear even when the rest of the paintjob is relatively intact above it. I use my *Dremel* rotary tool and impart some distressed rubber tire effects and then paint the inner surfaces with rust tones and redo the tire with greys and blacks to better replicate old worn out road wheels. The drive sprockets are then finished with lots of rusted surface since these were worn to bare metal and rusted fast and often.

The wheels had to achieve the correct look, and thanks to the fact *MENG* uses poly caps in their hub assemblies this really facilitates the painting process. Now I can get the pigments out and start to weather the lower hull sections.

LIMITED PIGMENTS
When studying the photos many of the tanks had old residual dried mud and this was great because the color contrast to the black lower

The process of applying the liquid fixer to the pigments, it's important to not touch them directly.

Because of the wet climate, I can further enhance the look of this derelict subject by adding some rust tones and green moss to the lower hull.

The *Friulmodel* metal tracks are assembled and test fit to the sprocket.

Stage One - the tracks are ready for the *Blacken-it* in the sealed container.

Stage Two - the tracks are placed in the container, *Blacken-it* is then poured in to completely cover the one assembled run, and then the lid is placed on tight.

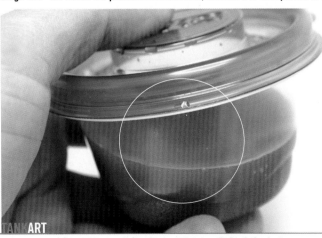

Stage Three - shake the container gently for 3-4 minutes.

tips on working with *Friulmodel* tracks:

• I learned years ago when I first discovered the amazing product known as *Friulmodel* that assembly is far easier when you use a stiff brass rod instead of the provided soft wire. The best size for most tracks are .020" brass rod that can be purchased from most general hobby stores or online retailers that supply such products.

• the reason to use brass rod (or similar) is so you can quickly push it through the pin hole with pliers and this will speed up assembly and provide a solid level of strength and tension without the need to add a drop of super glue on the end to hold the wire in place. Why? Well the next step I use (again another awesome product) is to soak the tracks in a weathering solution called *Blacken-it* (*AK Interactive* sells a similar product that does the same thing for international modelers), and the CA glue will not allow the solution to work properly and you'll get bare metal spots all along the pin openings.

thoughts on the using Friulmodel tracks and finishing them with Blacken-it:

• to further my thoughts on using *Friul* metal track sets and going with a solution finish versus paint is one I realized a long time ago. The main reason I go through this effort, (which does add some costs, I know), is because the final results are ***incredibly realistic*** and such that trying to get close via traditional painting methods is not such a simple thing. Sure we can paint them and do an amazing job, but compared to the real thing, this process gets extremely close nearly every time. Plus, it is not overly time consuming either, so it has an efficient element as well when one considers other link-to-link track set options. The resulting finish is also quite durable and once the tracks are mounted I now have a reliable handling point on all four corners, meaning I never have to touch the model's surface again. With that said, I try to incorporate *Friul* + *Blacken-it* whenever I can - they are a signature element on my models, in fact, I built this AMX-30 because *Friul* released a set for it finally.

The results after the tracks are dry. Note I created an asymmetrical finish, and from here I applied some rust washes and then painted the track pads black.

I try to create subtle asymmetries within the finishes whenever I can, and tracks are a great area to focus this unique effect on. I do this by varying the level of rust washes that I apply and consciously work within the randomness already in place from the *Blacken-it* process.

FRENCH MBT AMX-30B

Up next is to apply a pinwash to the larger joints and panel lines. This sets the tone for the weathering and gives us a base shadow effect for added depth.

The spare tracks are visually separated from the hull with a rust wash.

tips on weathering:

• each area of a model offers us unique aspects that we should be exploiting whenever we can. Here the spare tracks are a great area because of the fundamental lack of other original details such as gear or figures. Derelict vehicles require just as much thought as any other project and by focusing on details that we either increase the contrast to surrounding areas, or a different type of wear and tear, whatever can be possible within a flexible artistic scale-ism envelope.

On top of the pinwash I begin to apply dust and green moss tones using thinned *AK Interactive* enamels, which give the model an abandoned appearance.

thoughts on the preliminary weathering and how it translates to the overall final result: ●

• what happens during the course of the weathering is such a fundamental aspect to the entire project. But it's just as important that the early stages are well executed as the later. The buildup of the layers are when the mental transformation of us as the author happens and we can really begin to steer the final results to our liking and intentions. The AMX-30B represents some original processes, especially the addition of a green moss on the surface, something rarely attended to with armor models. As such, I can combine the dust and earth tones with the green moss tones and all this works to bring out a visual appeal on this NATO camo-schemed tank. It's that extra level of weathering that will make this model that much more unique and stand apart from other models of this era.

I continue this process to include darker earth tones and rusted metal areas. These are applied as transparent layers to continually buildup the opacity as I go.

OPR colors:
[clockwise from the lower left corner]

502 Abt.
• 130 Dark Mud
• 090 Industrial Earth
• 094 Green Grass
• 050 Olive Green
• 165 Faded UN White
• 001 Snow White
• 035 Buff
• 155 Faded 3-tone
• 092 German Ochre
• 093 Basic Earth
• 125 Light Mud
• 020 Faded Dark Yellow
• 110 Black
• 160 Engine Grease
• 015 Shadow Brown

Winsor & Newton
• Raw Umber
• Burnt Umber
• Burnt Sienna

NOTE: Place a small amount of each color on the cardboard and let sit approx. 30 mins to allow for linseed oil extraction.

Now is time to properly prep the oil paint palette for the OPR stages. Have a good selection of #2 Round brushes, plus flat rakes for the blending and streaking.

The process is similar in most areas, I apply extremely small amounts of oil that are then blended in.

thoughts on OPR:

• oil paints are such a powerful finishing tool that I can't overstate that fact enough. Make sure your cardboard palette covers all the colors of the model with 2-3 shades of oils for each tone so you can work as much depth into the paint as possible, within reason. For example, it is extremely easy to get carried away with rusted metal, so for most effects *less is more* is the best motto to follow. I always apply less than I need at first, and work up the tones layer by layer. I work *neat* and use very little thinner overall, blending is best done with a nearly dry clean brush.

• it's a very important aspect to respect the balance of the special effects from a compositional standpoint. In fact, it's sort of a technique in and of itself. It takes time and experience to intuitively be able to control the various elements at work. On this model, the volume and intensity of the rusted areas is of huge impact on the final result. It would be very easy to go overboard with the effect, and the stuff I discuss in the dedicated OPR chapters like brush size and the quantity of the oil paint applied are essential to achieving success with this stage of the game. On another note, I did take a moment and add some bird droppings along the turret basket railing, an influence from real life. These little details can be endless on a project like this, but one must always be conscious of the balance of these various details to create a standout model.

hull would be a nice visual enhancement. I was able to use *Wilder's* new line of pigments with the project and I made a small batch from four light tan and grey shades to recreate this effect. I didn't do anything different from my standard application process and I finish off the area with a judicious helping of surface rust and green moss, an aspect to this project that I really enjoyed incorporating into the final finish.

FINISHING TIME

With the basic weathering of the lower hull completed and the road wheels resplendent in their updated look, I attended to the Friul tracks to get them ready for final installation. As I explain on the spread detailing the process I used *Blacken-it* to arrive at a very realistic finish, from which I can apply some rust washes and then the rubber pad faces are painted an appropriate dark black rubber color, a very dark brown/green/black tone, and after the tracks are done I mount them one last time. One thing to note is that AMX-30 tracks show little to no sag at all, even the derelict tanks. So I had to glue the idler and drive sprockets firmly with CA glue to provide proper tension and precise fit, which took some effort to get on without damage. Like I said...for the final time!

The run to the end on this model revolved solely around the paintjob and getting the maximum from it to achieve the goal's of the project. Already the model is looking like the proper abandoned subject, but now I could really get into the patina aspects and pull out the enamels and oils. I start with a more traditional pin-wash and on the rear deck this helped a lot to give it some contrast. From that I then turn to the oils and methodically go around the entire lower hull, and then the turret. Using a broad spectrum of colors in the tan, brown, orange and green tones I was able to fully exploit all the painting efforts I applied earlier. The trick is to keep it in control, work one section at a time and move on. Once I attended to each area, then I can go back and work some areas a little more until the cohesive outcome is achieved.

thoughts on creating the overall visual effects while incorporating artistic elements:

• this part of the conversation is arguably quite subjective and prone to many levels of interpretation -- dealing with what is acceptable artistic license within a serious and historical setting. In this case, so few of you are true experts on the AMX-30 series I'm fairly safe in what has likely been overlooked in both construction and the final finishing details will go largely unnoticed. This was rather intentional because I knew that going in, there was room for me to express a more cohesive vision of these

The balance of this project hinged on how I interpreted the worn out paint effects as seen in the reference photos. There was a fantastic array of tonal shifts resulting from years of exposure, plus repeated paint jobs over the life of the tank, on top of which there was chipped and flaked off paint, causing a myriad of exposed rusted metal areas that all worked in concert to create such an interesting project from what is admittedly a less than popular subject. Let's face it we haven't seen a lot of AMX-30 built up models over time, even from the venerable Heller example. But times are changing and there is a resurgence in this era of armor and with the advent of the *MENG* AUF-1 155mm SPG kit release, we will be seeing a lot more of them moving forward. I say bring it on! I for one, can't wait until we get a proper 1/35 AMX-30 B2 Brenus.

derelict tanks versus the context of me presenting a Tiger or Sherman tank, or an M1 or T-55, as it were. By that I mean I can stretch certain areas more and flex my artistic muscles in my quest to create a piece that can still capture you, the reader, and offer up the necessary inspiration to tackle similar projects without upsetting a status qou. As the author, deep into studying this more obscure subject I can begin to manipulate elements at play to create a level of interest higher than even what the photos show. The trick to all of this was my mantra as outlined since TA 1, *scale realism*. By focusing on the results achieved by each special effect *in-scale* I have much greater room to maneuver and still turn out a piece that created strong visual interest and inspiration, while at the same time allowing me a strong level of processes to fully educate the reader in my techniques and those products that I'm using to realize the ultimate conclusion of this model. This in turn allows for a much greater amount of wiggle room of expression when tackling these less well known projects.

Remember when working with OPR, the model is already going to be telling us where and what to work on. The paint effects created with the HS chipping provides us with all the information we will require to be able to sit down and apply the oil colors to each spot. All of the wonderful marks made earlier now guide us to the finished result, and the efforts and stress level to achieve the right level of interest is far more controllable and enjoyable, which is the entire point.

Each section of the model was given substantial amounts of attention towards the complexity and depth of the paint wear. I couldn't neglect any exposed areas.

• I was really injected with enthusiasm as I worked on the finish here. It's not often a model can truly be relegated to a rusting hulk and this was as close as I've come while still having most of the paint present. I love how when you step back you simply see a well worn NATO 3-tone camo paintjob, but as you move in closer and closer the refinement within the paint wear, the near endless tonal variety to the three main colors and then the depth of the rust all becomes evident. I truly enjoyed myself, knowing I was creating a wholly unique model of a rare tank model.

• over the course of building up your model library, at least those that are completed, there will invariably be subjects that simply do not illicit that *wow!* factor, and the AMX-30 series sort of falls into that category. It simply hasn't seen enough action to headline newsworthy, even as much as I like it's style. Effort has to be made to search out a more unique aspect for it's finish, and thankfully someone felt it prudent to photograph the derelict tanks left to rot in the fields. This was a natural selection to paint the model as such, but with hopefully a follow-on AMX-30B2 Brennus in our future, there is a host of OPFOR's subject waiting to be painted up, even desert themed AMX-30's as well. One can hope...

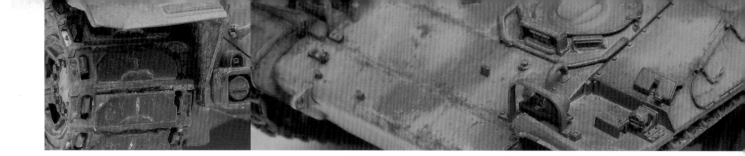

French MBT AMX-30B ●

It's a new age for 1/35 modern armor modeling, appropriately enough. It's a genre historically neglected by a lot of the major 1/35 kit manufacturers and in the last year (and looking forward), the amount of new 1/35 modern armor releases is and will continue to likely be a staggering array. I don't think it will let up anytime soon either since the bug has taken hold of a lot of us, and we are seeing so many new-tool kits being built online and for the contest tables it really invigorates this element of the hobby. Because WWII subjects are ultimately a finite group, modern armor has the advantage of always having new subjects appear. Couple that with some gaping holes for new-tool kits often overlooked in the past, and we are truly going to reap the rewards.

MENG is definitely leading the way, and their AMX-30 series has been a stellar addition. It takes a bit greater effort to research post-war French Armor because of the lack of quality reference material at hand, especially in English, but the end result of this extra work makes for some really unique pieces to add to the collection on the shelf. I, myself, have always liked the look of late 1950-60's armor in general, and those vehicles are often continually updated to extend their service life providing us with endless modeling possibilities. How could I resist a 1960's tank repainted multiple times then left out to pasture after its term of service was up? We all know that answer!

FRENCH MBT AMX-30B
1/35 MENG French Army MBT AMX-30B

FRENCH MBT AMX-30B

1 ASSEMBLY + TRACKS

2 REAR HULL MODS

3 TURRET CONSTRUCTION

4 GREY PRIMER

5 BLACK PRIMER

6 RUST LAYER

7 1ST HAIRSPRAY LAYER

8 BASE GREEN CAMO OVER HS

9 GREEN CHIPPING

10 2ND HAIRSPRAY LAYER

11 FADED NATO GREEN CAMO

12 FADED NATO BROWN CAMO

13 FADED NATO BLACK CAMO

14 NATO CAMO CHIPPING

15 WINDEX BARREL CHIPPING

16 PIGMENT PREPARATION

17 HULL PIGMENTS APPLIED

18 HULL WEATHERING

19 WHEEL WEATHERING

20 FINAL TRACK DETAILS

21 TRACKS FITTED

22 PINWASHES AND STAINS

23 OPR WEATHERING

24 FINAL WEATHERING DETAILS

07 BA 75

BRITISH FV221 CAERNARVON

1/35 Accurate Armour FV221 Caernavon

Caernarvon Prototype

This project had such a unique vibe to it from the moment I got my hands on the large box of resin from *Accurate Armour*. I have been a long time fan of both the Centurion and Conqueror tanks, and this model seemed such a natural fit to enjoy both at the same time. I mean how often do you ever see this model on the forums or at a show? I know I hadn't, so I jumped at the chance to work on this kit. But like a lot of resin kits, work it quickly becomes. Given the strength of modern armor as a genre in today's armor modeling hobby, I would not be surprised to see this very subject in plastic kit form sooner rather than later. In fact, those kit makers today that are cranking out these new kits should really consider the Conqueror line-up as viable kits for the future. I know I'd jump again at the chance to build the rest of the variants.

Even so, the *AA* kit is a beauty in its own right. It's very accurate, and all you need is in the box, so very little is required beyond dressing it with gear and figures, if that's your preference. From there, it is a lot about finding the right research on such an obscure subject. 50's armor in general always holds a bit of mystery to me anyway, the vacuum after WWII saw so much development, but not a lot of info has formally trickled out into our hands. There is basically one book on this particular subject and thankfully it is still readily available. So if you plan to build this project too, pick up a copy of Rob Griffin's **Conqueror**.

A WHOLE LOT OF RESIN

Even in this day of the Golden Age of plastic injected molded kits, there are still some subjects you can only get in resin. *Accurate Armour* has long supplied the hobby with a host of esoteric British armor subjects and this FV221 Caernarvon Medium Gun Tank Mk I is a perfect example of the breed.

The vehicle itself is one of those interesting development projects that had its roots in two different vehicles, the famous Centurion and the less so Conqueror. The British Army had decided to put forth two tanks to take on the might of the Russian Army at the time, and one that influenced many Western nations was the formidable JS-3 Heavy Tank. In response, the UK developed the Conqueror series heavy tank and due to a manufacturing delay in its turret production, the chassis was ready first. Because of this, it was decided to create a training vehicle that would bridge the gap between the existng Centurion units and those that were going to receive the much larger and heavier Conqueror. Enter the Caernarvon, a blend of the former's turret to the later's chassis.

Only a handful were completed but they provided an important footnote in the tank development of the era and this particular subject was used in extensive desert testing in the Middle East during the 1950's. I'm always looking for a unique take a project, and I realized the test tank was simply a quick repaint over the standard green base camo color, thus giving me the perfect opportunity to recreate some heavier wear and tear than would normally be seen on a regular peacetime test vehicle. In fact, I was lucky enough to find a photo of this specific tank during its desert test sessions, and apparently it completed over 3000 miles of desert testing and was then shipped back to the UK, which was how I planned to portray it. From this I could then replicate a much more interesting version of this already unique subject.

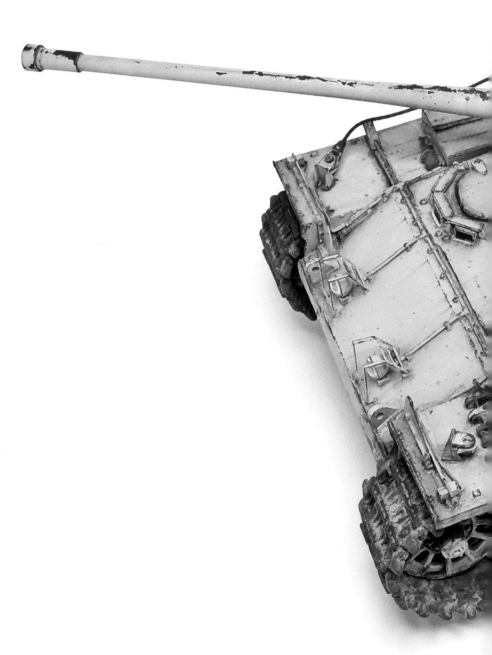

• every project will always have a series of challenging parameters, and we the modeler, have to find the path to an end result that will give us a more unique and original finish. We take on this challenge because when you have a kit such as this, with only a small amount produced, and no combat record to research and pull a myriad of ideas from, we have to turn towards other options. In this case, I was fortunate to have a choice between the standard European green scheme and this single desert test vehicle. I've long been a fan of desert subjects, so it was an easy choice for me, and once made, I then went about setting up a painting game plan to facilitate the execution of it.

Construction took place much earlier in the overall cycle of this project, one of the few mods I made were to trim the fenders and a couple of stowage items.

Like all good resin kits, the molded-in detail is visually superior and complete.

tips for working with resin kits :

• there are a couple of unique challenges to resin kits that differ from injected-molded plastic versions. The two major areas to concern ourselves with are warped parts and air bubbles. The former will require heat to help straighten the parts back to normal, and usually air bubbles (if present) are dealt with by placing drops of CA glue in each hole, and quick setting them with a CA kicker, then quickly sanding them flush. The better quality producers, such as *Accurate Armour*, built their reputation on superb castings and keeping these two casting elements to an absolute minimum.

• the other factor involved during construction is the common lack of mounting tabs, or locating pins, to help align the parts during assembly. Proper sanding prep of the resin, clean removal of the pour plugs, and dry-fitting are the essential processes to employ and ensure the kit goes together smoothly. In fact, with experience, resin kits can assemble faster than plastic kits.

thoughts on enjoying a full resin kit build-up:

• while it is admittedly becoming less and less common today, there are still plenty of opportunities to construct full resin armor kits. The need to kit up esoteric subjects continues to occupy a place in this hobby, and even if the plastic kit manufacturers are encroaching into this realm with similar releases of late, the list of what hasn't been kitted is still a very long one, giving the resin producers plenty to keep busy with. Sitting down with a box of resin, doing the prep work, and going through the assembly is an altogether different experience to gluing plastic together, albeit very enjoyable in own right. The satisfaction element can be much higher, and that alone continues to have merit.

TWO-STEP PAINTJOB

Not to overly state the obvious, but not every model paint-job has to ultimate, or best effort always. As we grow our collection of projects over time, we come across various elements that must be accounted for and here it simply wasn't going to a paintjob that rivaled the D9 Dozer 5 layers of complexity, for example. But therein lies the beauty of this hobby, and why it is such a constant stream of experiences that add up to so much enjoyment for us. I didn't have any undue stress on myself to recreate the absolute final word in desert paintjobs with this one, and thus I entered into the painting phase with a great attitude and knew I'd fully enjoy it and get a lot of satisfaction from its simpler outcome.

With that thought to keep it simple and straightforward, I chose a basic green in *Tamiya's XF-67 NATO Green* to start the painting off with. But as you are well by now about my penchant to prime my models, a full resin kit is pratically a must for a primer coat, and this time I used Gunze's

---

paint callouts for the Caernarvon project:

• 1950's BRITISH GREEN CAMO:
Knowing I would be applying a full coverage desert sand on top of the green, the ultimate accuracy of the green itself is not of paramount importance, and thus I went with a slightly lighter and brighter shade of green for this subject. I used the very versatile *Tamiya XF-67 NATO Green* as the base color.

• 1950's BRITISH DESERT SAND CAMO:
I envisioned sand camo of this era (immediately following WWII) to be quite light in tone, if not being essentially the same basic shades used during the war by the British Army. So I chose to go with *Lifecolor* on this project for the sand color and mixed a very light shade of tan colored camo utilizing *Lifecolor UA099 Light Stone* and *UA020 Isreali Sandgrey 67-73*.

quick ref:

• BASE GREEN:
XF-67 NATO Green

• SAND CAMO:
UA099 Lt Stone
UA020 IDF Sandgrey

thoughts on projects with less intensity:

• contrary to what some may think, even us professionals have to strike a balance between show pieces and those easier paintjobs that are both fun and less involved overall. As with the KV-1 in **TANKART 2**, this Caernarvon occupies that arena of a simpler, yet no less enjoyable project. Believe me, there is nothing wrong with that, and understanding it's not always about creating the ultimate piece with each model is always a good path to follow. Growth comes in all forms, and the less stressful subjects can help us achieve even greater success with our other models because you can have the chance to breath and remember why we do this hobby. It should be enjoyable on most levels. Call it a painting recharge, it keeps us fresh and ready for the tougher jobs down the road. There is a lot to be gained by flowing easily with a simple paintjob, it can free us from some of the classic pitfalls.

Stage One - primer layer via *Gunze's Mr. Resin Surface Primer*.

Stage Two - the basecoat of green is simple *Tamiya XF-67 NATO Green* sprayed neat. This is thinned with lacquer thinner to ensure a very smooth application.

Stage Three - the ubiquitous HS layer, full coverage is applied per the practice of two even coats.

dedicated *Mr. Resin Surface Primer*. This is essential because it will help spot any last minute air bubbles that may have escaped previous inspection. Now is the time to fix any of such issues, plus the primer is critical for proper paint adhesion on the raw resin surface. After that I cover the model completely with *XF-67 NATO Green*, which is arguably lighter than the actual 1950's green shade employed at the time. I need that extra lightness, if you will, because this will be the main chip color and they always appear darker in such cases due to the optical illusion of the small surface area exposed with each paint chip.

The next step is about as simple if hairspray chipping job as I have done to date. As I typically explain for the use of HS, I sprayed two even layers from

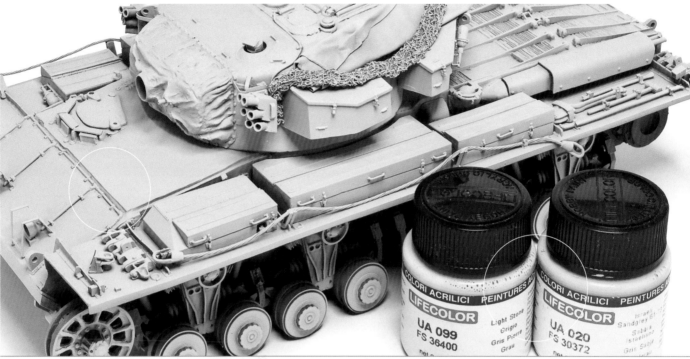

The top coat of desert sand camo is a simple mixture of these two *Lifecolor* paints, *UA099 Light Stone* and *UA020 Isreali Sandgrey 67-73*.

The chipping is created by scrubbing the top paint with a short bristle brush and water.

tips for airbrushing *Lifecolor*:

• effective airbrushing of *Lifecolor* acrylics is a rather common question still, mainly because it is regarded as one of the newer paint companies and many modelers are still discovering them. Plus, a lot of guys come over from enamels and trying an acrylic such as Lifecolor for the first time can be a little tricky.

• fortunately, *LC* paints are probably one of the most forgiving of the acrylic paints, and the simplest process for learning to thin them for airbrushing is to formulate an initial mixture of 50% and 50% water (tap water works well). Use that as a base formula for testing, set your airbrush to 20 psi and test spray on scrap. From here you then add paint, or water, depending on the outcome until you find the right mixing ratio balance for your specific setup. Everyone will have slightly different parameters in both equipment and environment depending on the season and your location. Just keep track of your test efforts as you dial in your *LC* thinning recipe.

• keeping this model low stress and sticking to a rather basic level of HS chipping was a good path to follow given the relative lack of quality references for this vehicle. It was almost therapeutic in my efforts to chip the paint, the process is controlled as I work around the model in small sections at a time.

• *LC* paints chip rather easily in the general sense of this process, but you do need to be cautious and make sure they are not overly large flakes, keep the amount of water used on the surface in check and work slowly. Let the chips flow from the sharp edges of the details and create them methodically as you go. It should not be a process that is rushed and ultimately the results will be a rather subtle effect that enhances the paintjob, tells the story better, and does not become the dominant factor. The chips should blend into the finish and be a natural element to it.

The chipping is subtle and integrated into the paintjob, I work very methodically to keep the results effective.

Once the HS chipping is completed, I spend time hand painting the smaller fittings and details. Sticking with *LC* paints keeps this process easy.

the aerosol can and let them dry completely, however, I speed the drying along via using a hairdryer on low heat. The main color is then applied and I used a very light tone of sand color mixed together from *LC UA099 Lt. Stone* and *UA020 IDF Sandgrey 1967-73*, and I am careful to apply it thin layers and build up the opacity very slowly. I believe *LC* paints are best applied in thinner layers and you will achieve a superior finish in this manner. This will also help with chipping in the next step, even though the top coat is rather opaque overall.

thoughts on evaluating the project and deciding the ultimate outcome of the paintjob: ●

• one of the many elements in play with any project is the evaluation of the painting progress as it moves along. While it's a great idea to have a solid game plan when starting, often times the project can come to an impasse, or deviate along another one (not often within our control, as hard as we may try!), which, in and of itself, can be a good thing. In this case, since it's a desert vehicle, the application of any earth effects is much less than a tank rolling around the plains of Europe, but I did have plans to really show some heavy paint chipping when I sat down with the kit. As I worked the HS chipping up to this stage, the model took on a look I was happy with and I decided to go a slightly different route and express a more subtle and less extreme outcome. Again, there is nothing wrong with that. Sometimes the opposite happens and a model calls out for a lot more extreme efforts, so each project will ultimately evolve as it goes along.

The detail painting continues with metal effect for the steel road wheels and idlers, followed by the decals.

An important step in the painting were the three small reflector lights. I used a layered combination of *Tamiya X-27 Clear Red* and *X-19 Smoke*.

tips for working the chipping:

• over the course of the HS chipping, the paramount importance of creating the effects *in-scale* are what I use as a guide while I scrub at the paint's surface. Usually, once the first initial signs of the lower color appear it is a good idea to move along and let that chip be. This way you can keep the smaller ones intact, and this is how you capture the right look. The trouble starts when you continually go back over an area that show chips. Once they start to appear the water will have a lot easier time getting underneath and that is when you need to be really cautious since the larger chips can form quite quickly, often without warning.

• use the sides of the bristles as a scrubber too, not just the tip of the brush. The act of the bristles rolling along on their sides has a unique effect and this is a great way to achieve a fine chip along the sharp edge of the armor. You can clearly see this style of chip in the photos on these two pages. Once I've created this base layer of chips, I can then pick and choose where I want the larger ones.

PRO TIP: You can never have too small of a chip!

tips on utilizing the chipped areas as a weathering road map: ●

• a relatively new idea that I've been concentrating on is the simple notion that if one was to follow a basic game plan of chipping early in the painting, than those areas begin to take on the element of a guide to help us further once we come back to weather the model and tie the effects together.

• the idea is obvious in its simplicity, and often it takes only articulating the thought to grasp it's power. What it does for us is to remove a large part of the stresses and pressures associated with trying to get the weathering "just right". We fight this element all the time, always striving to achieve the next level of whatever it is and ultimately this can drain us. Drain our motivation and energy to truly enjoy what we are doing. I think it's important to create a scenario in which each project we encompass the efforts as a pleasurable and rewarding process and I say that knowing a lot of you are not painters first and foremost. So with this simple idea of letting the HS chipping begin to create a map or guide for us to follow with make the next weathering stages a lot more straightforward and ultimately more rewarding.

PAINT WEAR & TEAR

From here the basic principles of HS chipping are applied, and I use a simple short bristle brush, a small cup of water and work my way around in a very controlled manner. I let the sharper surface details dictate where the chips appear and I utilize a light, yet firm controlled touch with the brush as I scrub across the model. *LC* paint chips somewhere in between *Tamiya* and *Vallejo*, so you will get some nice fine small chips, and occasionally a larger chip will form.

Once I have finished with the chipping phase, I quickly move on to adding some general weathering and begin working within the confines of the paintjob I've created and this helps facilitate a start to the weathering that fits with how the model is turning out. I wanted to maintain the lighter tones and yet still show enough usage that the model is interesting and tells the viewer an honest story of its short desert testing life.

• one of my favorite practices is to recreate layered rust tones, especially on exhaust systems. Something about it that makes it so much fun. Brings out the kid in me I guess. I discovered the power of *Lifecolor's* wonderful *Rust & Dust Diorama Paint* set a few years ago and have not looked back ever since I opened the first bottle. It's a simple and ingenious range of 4 rust tones that go from a light yellow to a really dark rust brown. The difference compared to regular paint, you might be asking, is the paint itself is more akin to a liquid pigment in that they dry to a very very matte effect that looks the most realistic of any rust paint I've seen in-scale. Often I see exhausts on models with heavy texture and like many such effects tend to be way out of scale. Rarely does the surface pits so severely in service life of a vehicle that you see really rough surface, it's often far more subdued than we imagine it to be. These *LC* paints capture the look just right, and are super easy to use.

• I prefer to thin the paints with water, apply the colors with a fine tip brush and simply hand paint the area I want going from light to dark with each of the 4 rust *LC* colors. In each application I maintain a translucent effect, and this is what creates the depth to the rust colors; the richness that you see in the final results. Once this process is complete, I then use a small piece of a sponge and only with the dark shadow rust color, add a few speckles of the darkest rust shade as the final element to the areas.

The exhaust and the spare tracks were treated to look like a lot of accumulated surface had occurred, which is a common look for exposed steel in the desert.

I layered the LC Rust paints in an effective manner, going from light to dark, then adding some light tones on top of the final dark colors. The HC chips provide a basic outline where to paint...

It was clear early on with this project that comprised of heavy steel tracks, large exposed exhaust system known for how hot it got and how much it rusted, and the general nature of the single color scheme that rust would be the perfect ally to use as a companion color and pop some needed visual interest into the finish. I spent time in the chipping to give the exhaust covers extra areas to rust, and then from there I simply used those chipped areas as my guide to apply the rusted effects via the *LC Rust* paint set, one of my favorite products.

I utilize these paints to recreate a heavily rusted area around each exhaust system and also with the spare track links. I carefully apply lesser amounts to the adjacent tools and tow cables, keeping the effect realistic to the task.

FV221 CAERNARVON

thoughts on working with a limited color palette: ●

• a unique aspect of painting and weathering to explore, especially with lighter color paintjobs, is to use a limited color palette for the total effect. By this I mean simplify your color choices for the paint colors, the pinwash, the oils and for the pigments. What this does is twofold; one, you are more efficient because of the fact there is less product to work with, and two, the end result can stand apart on your display shelf and become a more unique piece. The *less is more* effect in regards to painting.

• this project was ideal for such an effort, and I kept the weathering to a simplified scheme comprising of mainly rust tones, and a grimy dark brown color. It is just another of tackling the weathering and from this I could control the build up while at the same time challenging myself to make an interesting finish from less. It helps to have beastly tracks to pull this off and lend the model some substance via rusty tracks. The green chips give the model some visual depth, and the dusty and grimy surface is integrated for the overall effect.

WEATHERING BEGINS

I must admit this model really became a very enjoyable project at this point. So far, thing shave gone rather smoothly and no real hiccups occurred during the painting and chipping processes. Usually that means I can push right through the weathering and keep the creative juices going throughout! Never a bad thing. On this model, I wanted to pursue a slightly alternative form of weathering using a small range of tones for the actual grime and dirt colors.

There is something about how this turns out and I've seen other modelers intentionally do this to great affect, one in particular -- a small DAK Panzer I Ausf. A built by my friend Ulf Anderson a few years back came to mind and we talked about it one day, and I always kept that in my mind for just such a similar color scheme.

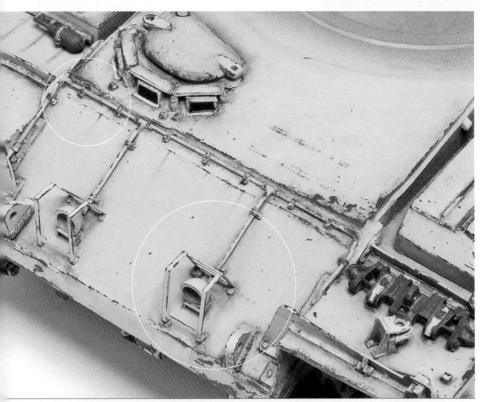

Rust stains must be handled with great care, a little truly goes a long way and subtle is always best.

I made efforts to impart a grimy dirt effect around the edges where the crew would frequently touch.

Having set that path in motion, I chose a few colors in the rust and brown tones for use to dirty up and give the paint some needed life and flesh out the details created to this point.

I bolster the efforts I did with the *Lifecolor Rust* paints on the spare tracks and tools by using a dark brown oil paint and working my way around the details with both a pinwash from it and some gentle color blending to give the sand camo some depth. I also use a rust colored oil paint and add very soft rust stains across the vertical and sloped surfaces and these are performed very cautiously and with great care. I use a new brush to ensure I can create the finest and softest rust streaks.

If I am critical for a minute, I think rust streaks are great visual aids, but often dominate a surface. Rarely is a vehicle covered with deep rich rust layers, but here we must keep ourselves in check. Like any other prominent weathering effect the in-scale appearance is paramount to its success. My application process is to use a very sharp #2 round brush, apply one tiny dot of oil to the base area where I want to start the streak, and then with a nearly dry (with thinner) sharp blending brush pull the oil downward and continue this until the color is almost invisible. That is when it look it's best, as seen in the top photo at the left. Believe your eyes will see any subtle color variation and when you achieve the near invisible stain, it's a thing of beauty! I can't help but emphasis the need to practice this small step, it makes a world of difference.

PIGMENTS

At this point in the project, I had to turn my attention to realistically presenting some form of dust to a certain extent. One of the hardest issues with a light tan colored paintjob is how to effectively represent earthen effects that correlate with the theater of its intent, such as a desert tank in a desert setting. It tends to be a tone on tone affair, and that itself is a rather unique challenge. Usually we have the added advantage of having a darker base color to play off of, thus giving the model some form of visual contrast to work within. Not so here, I had to carefully choose the tones of the pigments to achieve the right balance.

I was able to use the green color as a backdrop for the pigments and this allowed them to pop and I really went to town adding a ton of stains to the dried mud.

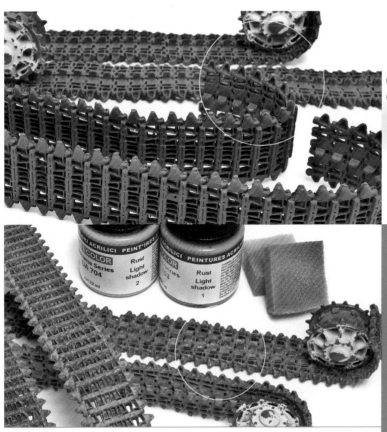

tips for painting heavily rusted tracks:

• again, another really enjoyable process for me is painting and weathering tracks. In times when I *can't* use *Friulmodel + Blacken-it* solution process, I like to try and replicate that style in essence with my painting. I start with a dark gray base tone, nothing overly specific, but I add dark brown and dark gray together and keep it stored in its own bottle. I usually pore excess grays and browns into over time so the color always changes from model to model.

• I switch to sponges and employ the same Rust paints that I used on the exhaust system. I thin the paint with water so it applies in a translucent manner, and unload the sponge on a paper towel first, then paint the tracks with them, always going from light to dark to build up the colors. This process adds depth to the rust tones and I finish them with pigments and some graphite.

tips to recreate the best random stain and splatter effect:

• oh, this tip is gold! I absolutely love using this effect and have developed a slight variation on this tried and true method of adding small spots in as random as possible manner. We strive constantly to create "randomness" in our work and this idea actually does what's supposed to. So the basic principle is this -- start with a dark oil wash, brown or black, or both is fine, using a fine brush like the usual #2 round, load some wash in it, then using a flat end of a tool (I use an old pair of tweezers), very gently flick the brush against the tool and spray the model in a very controlled manner, working your way around until your happy with the quantity. Simply very the amount on the brush for darker stains. The trick is being very controlled and use gentle flicks from only about an inch away from the surface, it's not a crazy heavy handed technique!

FV221 CAERNARVON

I used the rust tones of the tracks to help provide some needed color contrast to the model. I painted up a spare link run as well, but didn't use them after all.

thoughts on realizing the final weathering elements on the model:

• creating a successful project with the weathering is part of the challenge of working on a simpler model. The results can be just as effective and cohesive. You want a visually interesting end result that fits the subject and the intentions of the goals of the project. Here, I wanted a desert training prototype that had been put through its paces, but was not beaten up too bad, and was then sent home for final evaluations. I combined that goal with that of working within the confines of a more limited color spectrum for the weathering.

• even in this day of some more elaborate painting styles there is something challenging and interesting about a model like this, somewhat more straightforward and less flamboyant, but overall the skill sets get refined further by the artificial constraints set with the color palette. And it's a lot of fun too, I completely enjoyed the track and exhaust painting, the results came out great and as intended. Always a good thing!

There is a lot to still draw the viewer in closer to this model, the simple color scheme might even be missed at first glance on "the table". It's size and presence is helpful, but the very subtle weathering is a great tool to bring the viewer close and provide a lot more depth to the finish and help to tell a more complete story of this vehicle.

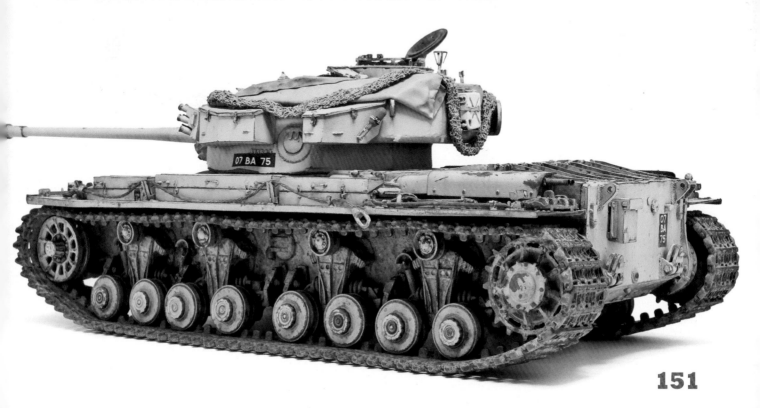

Ultimately, I used a mixture of *MIG Pigments* that were just a shade darker than the base color, which was essentially a mixture based around *European Earth, Gulf War Sand* and some lighter tones like *Beach Sand* with a hint of the greyish *Industrial Earth*. I used this primary mix down around the lower areas, and at least here I kept the lower hull side in their original green camo to give me something to work with. I applied only thin layer of pigments more for some visual texture more than absolute accuracy. Desert armor tends to not have large accumulations of dirt and sand due to the much lower moisture content, but certain areas and times of year could certainly alter that, and that was what I was after. As long as it looked believable. I also figured this tank likely moved slow and methodically and not at current MBT level speeds, so the dirt would stay in place better within those confines.

The real effort was the follow stains that I applied to the lower hull area. This is one of those oft looked over details that without, the model looks a bit too pristine to my eyes. I find the spotty nature of the stains adds a much needed grittiness to the weathering and I describe the effect on *page 147* accurately. Using some thinned oils and a fine tip brush, I flick it against a flat tool handle and carefully spray the surface with this dark thinned wash. From there it is just a matter of layering it up to get the right level of depth to it. The beauty is the various levels of opacity within each spot, that really adds to the randomness and natural look achieved.

FINAL DETAILS & TRACKS FITTED

From here I had just the tracks and final weathering to apply. I spend some extra time fitting the tracks carefully for the last time, resin tracks require some fine-tuned adjustments to get them just right, and I spot glued the upper run to the return rollers as a precaution so I can keep them looking tight with the hint of sag left in them.

My last bit of effort is to use some light tan and white oil paints to apply a thin dusting coloration to the tarps, the mantlet cover, the top of the fender storage bins and anywhere I thought to lighten the tones in a limited manner. Again the oils are so versatile, they become the final element of this project, a fitting tribute to this small footnote of Post-War British armor design.

The elements of tone within the sand camo itself are very subtly adjusted, somewhat like a gesture to Color Modulation theory. I've broken the expanse of the light tones with slight adjustments to each area in an effort to carefully give the model that lasting element of interest.

thoughts on the final elements that bring it all together:

• so much of what transpires over the course of a paintjob is dependent upon the skills we employ and can control, and level of precision of each process utilized. While I chose a specific weathering path for my finish on the Caernarvon, there is nothing set in stone in regards to what can and can't be done; for me, I simply focused on *scale realism* and made my end game about nailing the effects for my intended goals. If I can achieve the *in-scale* level I'm after, and bring out the story of the model then I'm usually pretty satisfied and feel I've done the project justice. Not everything we produce is going to be at the top of our skill sets, but everything we complete does add to our abilities and experiences, and that's where a lot of the true value comes into play for those simpler projects when you do not want or need to go balls out. It's a tough balance, I know we often want to take each project over-the-top cool, but it's not very realistic in the end, and the enjoyment factor can get damaged with that much pressure imposed on a constant basis. Being able to breath on some is of great value.

FV221 Caernarvon ●

The relentless expansion of the modern armor kit arena, especially in 1/35, has been a real boon to the hobby overall. I believe we are witnessing a rebalance occur on some level by showcasing that most new kit releases need not be WWII German in nature to be successful. Many of us that truly love this hobby know there are more vehicles still to be injected molded than we can likely recollect. 1950-60's armor in particular is a ripe arena, and as of this writing there are a number of very interesting kits set to debut. I know I'm very excited about what's coming out, and the chapter outline for the next **TANKART** Modern Armor book is going to continue to reflect the marketplace in this genre.

Accurate Armour is also a major part of the reasons why I feel this way, and they have always led the way, at least as far as post-war British armor is concerned. The *Caernarvon* kit is a beast in sheer size, and the *Conqueror* even more so with its massive turret and gun. But they need to be ready for more as we all know the plastic kit makers are starting to release a flurry of resin-like subjects and I look forward to what new kit *AA* produces for the modern armor fans out there. Either way, we are extremely lucky to have this broad level of diversity of subjects for us to build and paint for years to come.

07 BA 75

BRITISH FV221 CAERNARVON

1/35 Accurate Armour FV221 Caernavon

BRITISH FV221 CAERNARVON

1 PRIMER

2 GREEN BASE COAT

3 HS LAYER #1

4 SAND CAMO

5 HS CHIPPING

6 HS CHIPPING

7 TARPS & NET PAINTED

8 DETAIL PAINTING

9 MARKINGS APPLIED

10 MARKINGS APPLIED

11 RUSTED EXHAUST LAYER #1

12 RUSTED EXHAUST LAYER #2

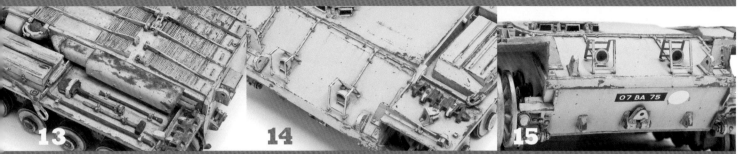

13 FINAL EXHAUST & TOOLS

14 FRONT HULL WEATHERING

15 FRONT HULL WEATHERING

16 PIGMENTS - DUST

17 DUSTING TOP AREAS

18 PIGMENTS - REAR

19 FINAL FRONT WEATHERING

20 TRACKS PAINTED - LAYER #1

21 TRACKS PAINTED - LAYER #2

22 FINAL TRACK RUST

23 TRACKS MOUNTED

24 FINAL TURRET DETAILS

RUSSIAN MBT T-72B (mod.1989)

1/35 Tamiya Russian MBT T-72B mod. 1989

T-72B mod.1989

The T-72. Low-slung and rather sleek I always thought, with larger wheels than it's T-64 stablemate giving it a greater sense of purpose, and the long barrel reaching out, this is the definitive Russian post-war tank, even more so than the T-55 series I believe. To me, I see the resurgence of the modern armor marketplace lead by the T-72 series, and the desire (or should I say demand) for new-tool kits of this subject is going to see us building a host of them in the coming years. It's the Panther of the modern era.

Given that, I knew the writing was on the wall when the first rumors that Trumpeter were going to give us a range of new-tool T-72 kits to follow up on their impressive T-62 and T-64 series; I had to build one in this book. It was one of the main focal points of this book being delayed, as it were, and while timing didn't play a good part for me to insert a *Trumpeter* T-72B (which are now out as you read this), the venerable *Tamiya* kit can still be made to look the part, given some extra muscle and a few bits of after-market accessories. Even armed as such, the necessity to have a T-72 in this book was a crucial element to address with the state of the hobby focusing on these subjects with ever increasing interest. It's my favorite tank subject in the modern arena and in it's final forms, the once incorrectly called *T-72BM* with its angular *Kontakt 5* armor array, has been a model I have waited a long time to apply a coat of paint to.

CONVERTING THIS KIT

Much has been written about *Tamiya's* venerable T-72M1 release. Now quite old in kit years, it has been the only viable 1/35 injected model available for quite a while (surprising to many of us, I'm sure), and the real story of this project actually goes back nearly 10 years now. Truth be told, even if I had somehow managed to squeeze the new *Trumpeter* release into this book, I'd have wanted to use this project instead for this chapter, largely for sentimental reasons. Let's face it, some shelf-queens just never stop calling to us, and finally the day had come to dust it off for **TANKART 3**.

But times have also changed a lot since then, and when I had originally started construction on this project details were scarce and limited regarding updating the early version the kit supposedly represented to the later and somewhat heavily revised B variants, in this case a mod. 1988 B-model, (a truly transitional variant). And I'll just lay out the disclaimer now, I know the model is not 100% accurate. Rarely are any of my models, and given the amount of details I changed or applied, it is at least a commendable attempt to represent a proper T-72B m. 1989. That said, if you were attempting the subject, I'd highly recommend the new *Trumpeter* release all day long and twice on model show Sundays... however, let me cover what changes I have done to this kit.

The model is to represent a *depot queen*, as I call it, that served in the Chechen War and had been knocked out with a HEAT round in the side of the turret. I don't build many battle damaged projects, but this one just lent itself to that notion. It gave me the excuse to remove all the fenders, which is a look I love on this tank. So the changes start with the road wheels. I used *Real Model* late T-72 resin wheels, which still hold up well, plus I kept a few of the earlier 8-spoke wheels to illustrate the subject's long service life. I then removed the front and rear fenders, save the left rear, and built the lower hull as stripped down as possible, especially at the rear, removing all extras like the fuel tanks,

thoughts on covering all the updates and mods necessary to be completely accurate:

• is that even a real possibility? I think for many of us, we try to balance it all out, but ultimately we have to deal with compromises at every turn, whether it is from lack of references, shortage of materials, to underdeveloped skills; all add up on projects of this nature. This is a subject I truly love and started this model in 2005, and it's been "on the shelf" for years, so when the time came to dust it off for **TA 3** I spent effort to update it using newer information to create a more accurate model. It's still a long ways from perfect, I make no apologies for that because this model is here to illustrate the paintjob for a modern era in-service Russian tank that saw intense urban combat action and suffered as a result.

the wood un-ditching beam, and the spare track links. I also filled in under the open sponsons (long a dreaded *Tamiya* trait), and cut off all the side skirt attachment points to prep for some minor scratch work in the end.

Now, the front end was an entirely different proposition. This was the one area that really stalled my build years ago and I had to wait until the release of one of the best resin update sets for this subject by *MiniArm*. Once released, I quickly snatched up the frontal armor set *#B35027*, but had to correct the *Tamiya* front glacis plate to proper B-model standards before installation. For this task, I used two-part epoxy putty to avoid any shrinkage, and then I attached the new resin nose piece. Once in place, I could set about adding the headlights (suitably modified to be properly attached to the headlight guards), the new electrical conduits and the missing weld beads. Under the nose, I scratched the four missing mine-roller brackets, however, in the fallout of it being an on-again/off-again project I overlooked the two locking flaps that keep the blade in place -- something gladly not an issue with the newer *Trumpeter* series of kits.

Scratchbuilt fender supports and mine-roller attached points were added from styrene rod and sheet.

The rest of the hull is set on adding some key missing details that really make the *Tamiya* kit sing and should be a rather standard upgrade for most variants. On the left side of the upper hull is what I suspect a long release rod for the smoke screen feature that runs in the gap between the left fenders and hull, this I made from various styrene rods and scratchbuilt pieces. And on the right hand side, the missing fuel lines are a critical omission, which was made from brass rod and some rubber tubing (using brass rod was important to create the large radi bend around the turret opening). The kit PE engine screens were added, and the taillight plumbing was the final details for the hull.

To the turret, which was completely replaced with the old resin *Terre Models* version and *Modelpoint Kontakt 5* armor set, and topped off with the *JS Models* and *DML* (don't ask...) stowage bins. Eduard's metal 2A46 125mm barrel completes the turret upgrade, and to finalize the look I removed the side smoke-dischargers in order to illustrate the battle damage better.

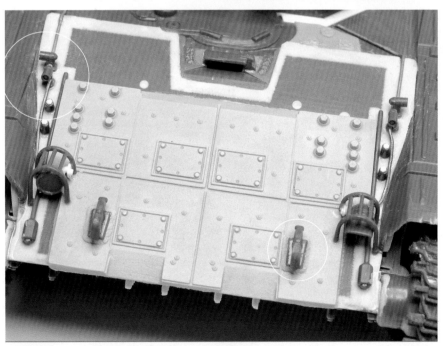

Electrical conduit was replaced with annealed brass rod, plus epoxy welds applied.

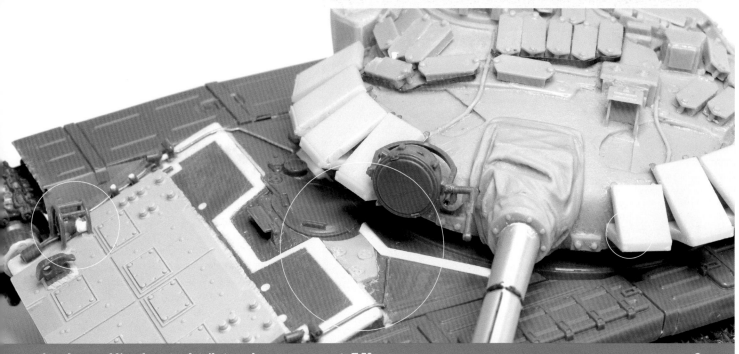

thoughts on adding the extra details to make a more accurate T-72:

• evolution dictates that we are never really satisfied with a project, and this is often more true before the paint gets applied. This model is an extended long-term project and when I picked it up again, it clearly needed to be brought up to current standards. To that end, I added the armored conduit covers on each side of the driver's hatch (which is still the incorrect A-model one), updated the frontal armor area to a much better level, and added new welds. The *Terre Models* turret is actually pretty good, but *MiniArm's* is definitely better detailed overall, and the *Eduard* 2A46 metal barrel with thermal wrap panels still looks very good.

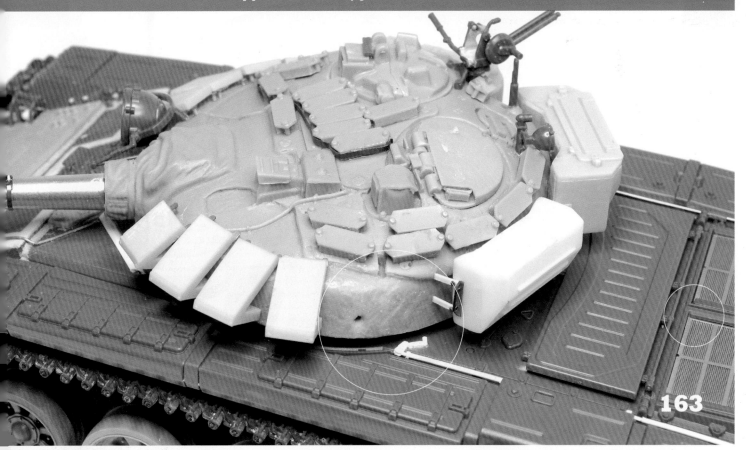

paint callouts for the T-72B mod. 1989:

• **1990's RUSSIAN PROTECTIVE GREEN NO. 2 CAMO:** For me, to accurately represent what is referred to as *Protective Green No. 2*, or *Protective Dark Green No. 2* in Russian Army practice is seemingly a moving target and requires a commitment to a certain shade you're after. We can typically struggle with accurate WWII shades, this range of greens is no different, and appears to shift depending on time frame of application and length of service (and/or the action the vehicle has seen). I wanted to represent the richer darker green shades of this modern era color and used *Vallejo Model Air #223 Light Green & #225 Green* from their *Russian 4BO Paint Set* for the lighter tones, and for main base color I used *Vallejo Model Air 71.017 Russian Green.*

quick ref - Vallejo colors:

• BASE GREEN:
017 Russian Green

• LIGHT GREENS:
223 Green
225 Light Green
(from Vallejo Russian 4BO Paint Set)

MODERN RUSSIAN PAINTING

I stepped forward into this paintjob with quite a bit of enthusiasm. I've not had a good clear opportunity to tackle this era Russian camo colors before, and somewhat ironically, the paints chosen were actually intended for the WWII vintage subjects. Be that as it may, I tend to not get hung up on the label names of any products, they exist largely for marketing purposes, and I will target colors based on very specific avenues I am seeking to explore. In other words, because I was going to use *Vallejo* acrylics for this model (for a couple of reasons), I was going to choose from their range. First of those reasons was that it's been a while since my last *Vallejo* paintjob, and since that time I've now coordinated a new sponsorship program with them and want to illustrate their range of products in my work. Thus, when I set about to select the right colors, I used the greens I felt were going to give me the most success. That is how I select each product I use in fact, the end results are my guiding elements, not so much what the label says.

Stage One - primer layer via *Vallejo's* new acrylic *Surface Primer*, a light grey in this case.

Stage Two - working with the *Vallejo Chipping Medium*, I sprayed the model in two thin even coats.

Stage Three - the red primer is mixed with *Vallejo Model Color 957* + a few drops of *982* added.

thoughts on layering monotone schemes: ●

• this project was destined to become the true monotone camo scheme in this book, and from there I wanted to embrace the challenge of pushing myself to apply the same level and depth of finish to this model that I had previously achieved with the D9 and T-62M1. Studying modern Russian armor photos, there is certainly a relative level of paint wear associated with their extended service lives, and their use in the smaller 20th Century conflicts of Eastern Europe. Red primer is prevalent, as is various forms of paint chipping, thus, using my experience, I determined a path of colors and products that would achieve this level of finish to the highest standards.

With that thought working through my head, I was able to lay out a plan for what I felt was a far more intricate presentation than the seemingly simple monotone camo was indicating. Monotone colors are actually never really that, singular, and in essence I was about to go full bore into a very layered painting process, not unlike any of the other multi-colored projects presented in this volume. And to follow my current practice of experiencing newer products available, I set my trusted *Gunze Mr. Surfacer* primer aside to try *Vallejo's Surface Primer*. I'll say beforehand, I know there is a trend to introduce colored primers, but I believe the light grey shades are still superior for the purposes of priming to inform us of the quality of the prepared painting surface. I simply prefer that color choice and sprayed the model with it (I used the *Surface Primer* from their new AFV Painting Set *German Dark Grey #78.400*).

With the primer sprayed, of which I had zero issues, the model was for the first time (since I began this project all those years ago), looking like a cohesive vehicle. Primer coverage was great, and the surface was impressively smooth, and all I did was squeeze some into my airbrush cup, add a couple drops of thinner and sprayed the primer at approx. 20psi. From there I quickly moved to the *Chipping Medium* fluid that I sprayed in two even layers, same as when I use HS, and then applied the first round of color, the red primer undercoat. I looked closely at a lot of reference and red primer is actually quite commonly seen under close inspection of T-72's. I went with a bright red, for a touch more contrast because the chips would be exceedingly small in the end. I will put forth a concentrated effort to keep this extreme paint wear effects in-scale, which is as always, my primary goal with such elements.

165

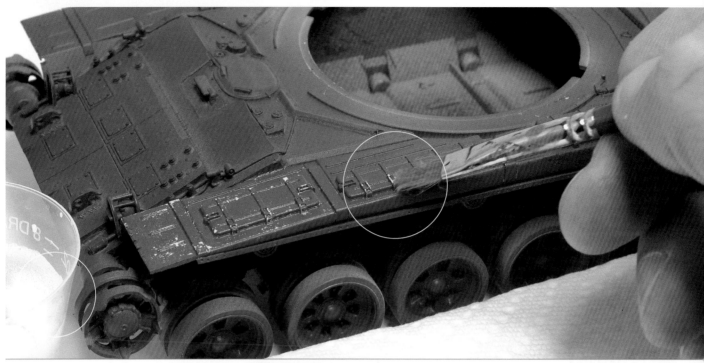

Chipping with water and flat brush with splayed bristles is following along with the exact same technique as HS chipping...very nice results are achieved as well.

The extensive chipping results from the myriad of tiny raised details on the surface.

tips for chipping with Vallejo:

• basically the main types of acrylic paint that I employ chip with varying degrees of styles and success. In truth, *Vallejo's* are the hardest type to control due to their nature as a vinyl acrylic, which creates a shell and thus large flakes can and will occur. This is countered by forcing yourself to monitor the thickness of each paint layer and really maintain thin even layers of paint when spraying *Vallejo's*.

• also, in specific regards to using it for chipping with a chipping product like HS or the dedicated *Chipping Medium*, it works better to thin the paint a touch more than normal with water. *Vallejo's* already react very well when thinned with water, and frankly you must do some quick practice runs to achieve the right ratio. It does vary a little, but I tend use a lot of *Model Air* colors, so they naturally require less water than the much thicker *Model Color* range. I test this by wiping the mixing brush along the edge of the cup and watching the paint drop run down, it should move quickly indicating it's properly thinned. That will help keep your paint layers thinner, and provide a better quality of paint chip with *Vallejo's*.

thoughts on chipping: •

• I knew up front that I'd be layering colors and the *Chipping Medium* in between to fully explore this process to the maximum. Part of it was to compare this product to the HS process, and in truth, the results are nearly identical overall, it just requires the use of an airbrush to complete vs. the aerosol can. My extensive chipping experience certainly helped to guide me, as it were, and I know what factors can cause issues regardless of product. Too thick paint is one, and not enough chipping product another. I was steadfast in applying the *Chipping Medium* as two light and even layers, drying them in between, same as the HS. I cover the model accordingly to make sure I have product everywhere I'll need it, and then I can set about to apply the next base colors in a very controlled fashion. Control is key with each step we take, chipping or otherwise.

The red primer is then covered in a single layer of satin varnish, followed by two thin even layers of *Chipping Medium*.

The next round of spraying focused on applying a mixture of dark and lighter green tones to help break up the model according to ref photos.

167

thoughts on incorporating *Color Modulation* in a more restrained manner with this paintjob: ●

• we have such a wonderful array of finishing ideas to employ with each model, it's good to evaluate early on and determine which ones will achieve those results that satisfy your own goals as a modeler, and those of the model. I speak of this task often, it's integral to any project's success and here I had my latest round of challenges to fully illustrate a depth of finish I was seeking that would both elevate the craft and create a much broader interpretation on painting single colors schemes. Color Modulation is a very powerful tool, and like all great ideas, it's true relevance is found in it's ability to be applied with success in vary degrees of intensity. I was after depth, not dramatic effects, and thus I set to the process of varying the panels of the model in accordance with my own experience and studying reference of both this vehicle and similar tanks that have such a variety of panels to incorporate the concept upon. This idea was facilitated by *Vallejo's* brush painting qualities. They are capable of wonderful color transitions via thinned layers, and this is the *how* of what I did above. I used the broader spectrum of greens and set about to break up the surface panels and details in this manner.

Explained at right, I swapped one technique for another when I hit a snag, the results are largely the same.

One benefit of the switch to the acrylic thinner removal technique is that I can subtly wear away the light green to show fresh dark green underneath, which is a very common sight with modern paint formulations that hold up well over time. The faded top coats wear off showing fresher paint.

when things go wrong:

• it happens...more than we all like to admit. I'm writing this section to intentionally discuss that problem, what went wrong and why -- and how I set about to fix it, switch techniques and move forward with success. In short, the water could not penetrate what ended up being vary opaque layers of green to allow me to chip the *Vallejo* paint effectively. I violated my own rules about applying thin paint and this was the result of the trouble I had properly covering the bright red primer. I backed myself into a corner and *Tamiya* paints tend to work better for such situations, and the vinyl sheel effect of *Vallejo's* appeared and caused a change in plans.

• knowing the *why* and *how* to fix it and move on is a critical element to success with any project, and this issue was so glaring I felt it important to highlight it. So the solution -- I switched from water chipping to acrylic thinner paint wear that I discuss in **TANKART 2** with the M26 Pershing chapter. I essentially sidestepped the chipping issue and proceeded to wear away the green paint with *Tamiya* X-20A thinner (which is very stable and controllable) and this allowed me to carry on with the worn effects I was after.

tips for success using thinners for paint wear:

• so how does the process actually work, and what is the best way to achieve the proper results? Using thinner to wear away a layer of paint is nothing new, and the resulting effects can create an authentic finish where the desire to illustrate the age of a vehicle are of importance. It starts by having multiple layers of color already applied to the model, and then with an older brush you gently rub away the top layers of paint with very very small amounts of thinner, similar to dry-brushing in it's method of brush control.

• anytime you employ this concept, the most important element to success is how much thinner is being applied. The secret is to use as little as possible to achieve the result. It starts by unloading the thinner from the paint brush. I keep a paper towel beside the model and once I dip the brush into the thinner, I wipe most of it off until the brush is nearly dry. From there it is critical to work in small sections, like dry-brushing, very slowly and skim only over the upper surface details to remove the top layers to create the effects and chips. Control and practice are fundamental elements that must be heeded.

PAINT WEAR & TEAR

It is at this time in the painting process I experienced my first hiccup of note in a while. I have admittedly had a smooth run of paintjobs, and two things happened here that are worthy of mention. I'm a firm believer in learning from mistakes. I unfortunately not heeded my own advice and applied too opaque of a green top coat and the nature of how *Vallejo's* dry as a vinyl shell prevented me from fully exploiting the *Chipping Medium* process once I applied the camo colors. Because I spent so much effort modulating the panels and tinting the various greens, I ended up applying too much paint and this didn't allow the water any way underneath to effectively chip the paint off.

I knew it almost as soon as I tried to use the water, and fortunately I had enough experience in hand to know to rapidly switch techniques and not lose much, if any, time. Definitely not the way the plan had been worked out.

thoughts on adjusting the plan: ●

• I'll be the first to admit not every model goes exactly as planned. There are many times during a project adjustments need to be made, some small, some big. I didn't really experience a problem with the paint per say, just that the ability to derive the results I was after had to be altered to achieve the look I wanted. It's why I'm writing these books, in large part because this discussion becomes more commonplace and even the best of us must walk a path that contains obstacles. It's why these models are so challenging, and for me it helps to refocus my efforts and push myself to the higher levels I'm looking for. All of which gets put into the memory files and the next project(s) can benefit from this gained experience.

The canvas mantlet cover and anti-radiation panels were handpainted with the appropriate shades.

The excess paint wear was created with the *thinner removal process* and it allows all the colors to become part of the layered paint chip effects, which was the ultimate goal, regardless of the technique used.

The main turret markings were applied over a coat of *Chipping Medium* and *Eduard* stencils were used for the numbers themselves. I used some thin strip of Tamiya tape over the stencil to split the "8".

To continue the paint wear I switched to using *Tamiya X-20A* acrylic thinner for my primary paint chipping process. It does a very commendable job as it is, so I quickly got past this mistake and fell into the groove of wearing off the top colors with the thinner instead. It actually went very well, and by maintaining my discipline and control over the technique I was able to achieve the desired results.

With that hurdle overcome, I could now effective paint the anti-radiation panels on the turret and the small one by the driver's hatch, and paint the canvas mantlet cover, again using *Vallejo's* to brush paint those areas. Afterwards, I applied the white turret markings, and typical of my models, I went with a completely random unit number and worked with reference photos to create a close approximation to current Russian Army practices. Here I was at least able to redeem myself somewhat and use the *Chipping Medium* again with the turret numbers to achieve a chipped paint effect.

RUST CHIPPING

With the model starting to come alive and be much more representative of the project goals, the next element of painting was to add some rust chips. Typically, an in-service modern era tank would exhibit very little rusted areas, but due to the nature of the subject and my portrayal of it as having been sent to the maintenance yard after being knocked out, I could add some rust chips per the ref. photos I was using.

The rear rubber fender flap was treated to some light dust washes to start its weathering.

For this element, I decide to use the sponge chipping technique to apply rust chips in a very controlled manner. I like how *Lifecolor's Rust* paints work in this instance so I grab my set and small sponge pieces and proceed to apply tiny rust chips to very specific areas, like the tow hooks, exposed fender edges, fender stowage straps (note the fuel tanks and fender storage bins are made of alloy, but the straps are steel), and some of the various edges likely to be worn normally and then rusted after sitting idle for a while.

PANEL FADING

The ability to create the overall worn paint effects in a realistic manner had dominated the efforts to this stage, but I clearly had more effects in mind and how best to represent them in paint before I get to the even more involved OPR stages. I wanted to impart a slightly more distressed element to the green camo without resorting to airbrush fading, so I decided to apply very thin layers of heavily thinned acrylic paints to the myriad of panels across the surface. *Vallejo's* are ideal for this technique because of their figure painting qualities, and they perform beautifully in such circumstances.

I start, like most of my methods, in one small area of the model and slowly work my way around, usually the right front corner (just my habit it seems). I am always conscious of the cohesive effects as a whole, and work the panels in

The overall stance of the model is starting become more evident, and I continue with the paint chipping wear down along the running gear.

tips for sponge chips:

• because of the fact that I had to switch chipping techniques previously with the green camo, it also meant I had to readdress the way I wanted to portray the rust chips. Remember this tank was a depot queen sitting in the maintenance yard for a while after it was knocked out of action. Thus all the worn exposed steel areas would quickly rust in the moist European climate.

• I enjoy the *Lifecolor Rust* set, the paints are true matte and this helps achieve a nice contrast with the glossier camo. It works best to use the lighter tones first to establish the area for the chips and then apply the darker rust colors on the highest areas, or in the center of the larger area as a whole. This creates another visual layer to the effects, more realism and interest.

• again, it is highly recommended to *always* unload your brush, and the sponge is no different. If you dip it in the paint and apply it directly to the model, it will be a mess. Instead, *always* unload the paint onto a paper towel first to almost the point that the sponge is dry, then you can apply the paint to the model more effectively.

Working with sponges for chips is like anything else, always unload the sponge prior to applying it to the model.

With the sponge unloaded, I use tweezers to hold the small piece and gently stipple the areas I wanted to have the rust chips in a controlled manner. **173**

Layers of rust tones are applied in a very thinned and controlled manner to edges of the fenders and the various bits chipped and exposed to the elements.

I work the sponge chipping on all the steel parts, always using the paper towel to unload the paint.

tips on sponge chipping:

• a couple of additional tips for working with the sponge is remember to clean the sponges after a while of use, because they too can get too much paint build-up and you'll lose the smaller more refined marks from the tiny sponge edges.

• also remember to rotate the sponge as you work your way around the model, or better yet use multiple pieces to stop from creating a repetitive chipping pattern, which is one of the more common pitfalls when using this technique. It becomes very easy to simply hold the sponge as is and dab the surface, the problem is you start to repeat the marks and this looks very artificial and can be quite easy to spot. I typically employ 2-3 small pieces of sponge and often switch them out.

thoughts on panel fading: ●

• this is a wonderful and rather fun process to use when you want to further break up some of the surfaces. Thinned paint is essential for a tint, otherwise you end up repainting and that is likely too strong of an effect. Thin watery layers are more effective to achieve the end results -- layers!

• layers are key, slowly slowly build up the effects, and because it's an acrylic, *Vallejo's* here, it dries fast and the process itself is not long to complete. Just don't rush it in other words.

• like nearly all methods that employ thinned products, have a paper towel handy -- the single most important element to success is learning to properly unload the paintbrush prior to applying the product.

The panel fading is achieved with very thinned down paint and a good brush, always unload on a paper towel prior to applying.

Another look at how this step works, note the paintbrush is not overly wet and the amount of tinting is kept in total control. This is key to achieving the right results. Layering the tints over previous effects adds depth and creates a more subtle finish that enhances realism.

thoughts on realizing the transitional painting to weathering elements on the model:

• there comes a moment in the processes where we make the switch from painting to weathering. I tend to concede the idea that weathering is essentially how dirty an object is, and try to keep painting, even the wear effects in a separate discussion. I do this mostly for efficiency and having an clearer time discussing the two processes, which hopefully makes it easier for you, the reader, to understand what it is that I'm trying to accomplish with each paintjob. With that said, this stage here is just about the moment of transition. Typically I see it as the

point where the model is telling me its story in a very clear vision. So much effort has transpired to this stage, I can easily imagine the end results and this allows me to focus on making what I've created *dirty*, in simplistic terms. Of course, the theater of action, time of year, and some other larger variables will determine to what degree this happens, but the fundamentals of the model's finish are in place. And this is how the theory that the painting and chipping efforts create a road map for the oil paints and what comes next, followed by the pigments. The more this conversation gets expanded upon, the easier it will be for the concept to take hold and create a clearer path for others to follow along. From the images here, I'll now unleash the full compliment of OPR techniques onto the surface, taking it to the ultimate levels I can imagine.

The rusted effects are carried out where the battle damage occurred, along the side skirt bracket and exhaust.

such a way to impart realism yet increase visual interest and appeal at the same time. This is what elevates the model from a simple monotone project and on to something that will draw the viewer in closer and create that level of interaction we are after.

I do this by taking lighter shades of the *Model Air* green camo, thinning them down to almost 50-50 with more water and then with my #2 round brush, I unload the paint first and carefully brush a wet coat onto the surface of the panel. It dries quickly and I can see the tinting taking place, I apply more if needed. I'll be able to alter and adjust this effect even more with the oils, and I'm creating a greater level of depth to the entire model by using this technique now at this stage.

Why? Well, the T-72 in particular is actually a very busy model, the surface is covered with many "panels", there really isn't a lot of clear open painted metal like the M1 Abrams, or a T-34, for example. Stuff is everywhere, so it works to our advantage to create as much variety within the paint now. We are essentially combining the chipping effects with the painted panels as a road map for a much more efficient OPR stage to follow. It's a smarter path to better results.

OIL PAINT RENDERING (OPR)

From here on out, the model began to really illustrate the worn-out tank I had envisioned early on. I could now turn my full attention to maximizing the paintjob and move into the advanced stages of extracting all that I can from this project. Turning

thoughts on focusing efforts:

• to this point the model has been a procession of layers, effect upon effect, and this brief discussion is just a simply reminder of the relevance and importance of continually applying this layering concept within each step as you attend to the painting and weathering. Restrain from trying to achieve it all in one go, strive to use less product more efficiently, control the chips, and push yourself to create *in-scale realism*.

The layers of thinned green paint are aided by additional elements of paint wear, and the darker green areas resulted from rubbing the light green off with X-20A thinner.

thoughts on the mental levels and efforts required to continually strive and achieve more:

• the theory that we as the authors can maintain a strong and focused semblance of control throughout the project is a key area of our mental recognition to continually pursue the end result in a rather relentless endeavor. None of what you see in the pages of the **TANKART** series comes about as easy, or without lots of practice and forethought. To achieve, we must invest ourselves at each step of the project. We must evaluate ourselves, alone most times, at the bench with our reference at hand and the products strewn about the work area. We have to sit and ponder techniques, products, methods and quantities in a variable stream of processes to see these models completed. But here's the thing, and it's a good thing. The more we do, (like anything else) -- the better we will become. The models will be better, your control of the airbrush will be better, the brush strokes will be better, you will be better. Above, the model begins to take a distinct turn toward what I had always envisioned for it. My efforts, including my missteps are brought forward together through continual efforts. The many layers of patina are coming to the forefront and now the life of the vehicle, its story, is starting to be told. And one of the most important elements for model building success is being a good story teller.

The OPR palette is created with a broad range of oils to cover the base greens, the rust areas, grease and grime, and all the initial dust layers I want to apply.

thoughts on working with OPR to illustrate the maximum potential within the paintjob: ●

• it's important to remember there is no preset technique when with working oils, rather it's the variety of layers that we apply and the ability to alter each one and vary the opacity and concentration of color. Oils are remarkably forgiving, and I like to start slow and work up my pace as I go. The first sections, more or less, will dictate the rest of the model, so I focus on these sections and try to fully maximize the effects I can apply. I will typically start with lighter shades, and go darker, and I fully realize each section before I move to the next one.

• one reason that I suggest creating your palette with approx. 2-3 shades of oils for each "color" is so we have some options. There is no reason to limit your selections, especially as you build up your oil paint stash. Remember they will last a very long time and are a fantastic investment for modelers, one of the most cost effective medias we have available to us. The ability to control their opacity is utterly fantastic!

One of the more effective processes is to gently flick paint onto the surface to further break up the monotone panels. It can also act as a unifying element across multiple sections because it subtly ties them in together. My method is very controlled, very. I work close to the surface and flick small amounts of various colors to both add various stains and spots to the paint, both dust and dark oil stains. But the key is to limit quantity and distance so it refined and applied with control.

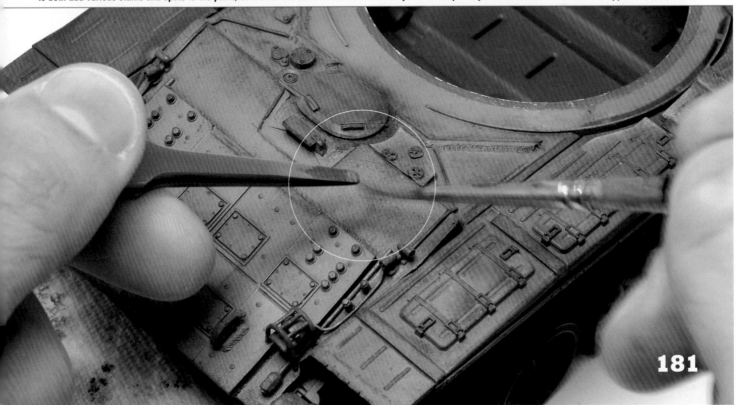

tips on using OPR and getting the best results at this stage: ●

• when a project reaches this stage, the conversation between you and the model changes. What occurred up till now has essentially created a framework for us to evaluate and maximize, and the best tool in our arsenal are the oil paints. They are incredibly powerful and provide a staggering array of possible effects. The opacity levels being a crucial aspect to them, and that leads to a maximum level of control for each layer of application.

• for the full effect we must study the reference photos, pick a good starting spot and slowly begin to work the oil paints into the surface. By varying the opacity and quantity applied you can control what sort of effect achieved -- from very thin dust layers, to full blown oil and fuel leaks. On top of this, I try to impart as much paint discoloration into the model as I can without going overboard. Again, that fine line is easily crossed, but I try to give the illusion the crew used the vehicle, or combat has adversely affected the paint, and like a mechanic caring for an old friend's car, his "fingerprints" are all over the place. So in essence, I combine the two goals as I work over one small section at a time. By doing it this way, I cover both the natural results of weathering, plus those more man made visual paint effects.

to the OPR process was essential and I created my palette of oils to cover all the colors I intended to utilize. My goals were to enhance the rusted and chipped areas, to add the initial layers of dust and dirt accumulation and some general staining to give a greater sense of use by the crew.

To exploit the battle damage on the left side of the turret, and for the other effects I had to study the reference photos very closely. It is very easy to get carried away and be more of an artist than a story-teller; it's a fine line that gets walked in such cases. For example, I wanted to show the gritty residue of urban fighting from dirt and bricks falling onto the top areas, which leave a certain style of mark. Plus, I wanted to enhance the different materials of this vehicle such as the textiles, the alloys, and the steel, which all have specific properties. I wanted to truly bring out as much depth to the main green camo colors on top of all of this effort, so I concentrated within each section the varying dust and dirt elements alongside the green discol-

• what do I mean when I say varying the opacity and quantity applied? First the opacity. What I mean by this is when you put the brush into the oil typically you only use a very small amount and often some thinner is used to alter how opaque (solid vs. translucent) the oil will be. For example, for thin dust I often have a wetter oil brush and then work the dust colors into the brush on the palette, even dip it in the thinner a touch more, dab the paper towel to unload the brush then work the oil into the surface. Note I am referring to the oil brush so far, not the blending brush, which I haven't used just yet. In this manner, I am controlling the opacity of the application via thinner and amount of oil on the brush.

• for the quantity aspect, I am referring to the volume of oil applied to the model, rather than how much oil is on the brush. True, I need to have oil on the brush to add more to the model, but I can keep doing that until I have the look I want (even varying the amount of oil on the brush during this step). For example, to use the dust scenario again, say I wanted a thicker more textured area, I would apply more oil to the section using less thinner in the process to build up the color and thickness with more layers.

• blending brushes are usually kept clean and nearly dry in both regards, which helps to control the effects better.

Each painted effect already in place is gone over with OPR and enhanced to its maximum potential, while still maintaining a common level of balance over the entire model.

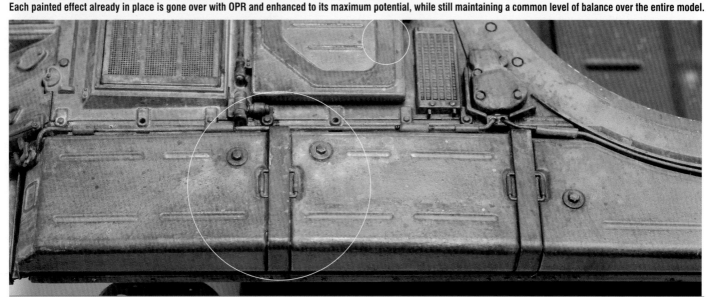

Working the oils between the various colored panels, I maintain both the color separation and the cohesive visual appeal across the surface. At the same time I am able to create very subtle tonal shifts across the same section, so the depth and variety of effects becomes even more layered.

tips on applying pigments to the lower hull:

• the mighty pigments -- they have transformed weathering in my opinion, and elevated our craft to much greater levels than pastels ever could. I'm a fan! Each project has a specific goal, and the earthen effects are almost always a very critical element. Typical of my work, I usually model in-service tanks, but here this one is representing a depot tank that has sat for likely weeks on end without moving. For me that visual is different to an active vehicle in that the mud and dirt will have long since fully dried, and the color is more uniform as a result.

I create this effect by combining four of the new *Wilder* pigments to make a suitable light dried mud color with a distinct greyish tint typical of urban environments, and I blend them into a 35mm film container. My usual application practice is to then place the hull on its side and proceed to add rather thick and generous layer of the mixture. I'm not shy with how much I apply because I'm after a thick dried and cracked appearance, indicative of old dried mud. To achieve that specific effect, I set them in place with equally generous amounts of *Tamiya X-20A* thinner using a eye dropper to facilitate the procedure. If I use too much and the thinner is pooling, I take an old brush and suck some back out; this way I control the level of thinner applied. From there I dry everything with a hair dryer on low heat to make it crack, as seen below.

finishing tips for the *Friulmodel* tracks:

• working with *Friulmodel* tracks is one of my favorite practices, I love how durable they are and when coupled with *Blacken-it*, the finish can be as realistic as possible. I can then enhance what that's created by applying a few other products to further the look I'm after. Because of the inactive nature, I wanted more fresh and dark rust and none of the bare metal showing. Using the same pigments as the hull

from *Wilder* I started by adding them dry along the outer cleat faces. Again, like the hull, I'm generous with the application and this look follows what I'm seeing in my reference photos; to achieve the dense dried-mud appearance I need a lot of pigments. I set those with some *X-20A* thinner, just as before, and then dry it that all at once. After that, I can attack the tracks with the rust wash, *AK Interactive's Light Rust Wash* in this case. With one simple general wash layer added the tracks provide a wonderful variety of rust tones because of how the *Blacken-it* treats the surface of the metal. Again, I dry the tracks with my trusty hair dryer, and for the final element, I switch to *Lifecolor Rust Dark Shadow* and using a small piece of sponge I dry-brush all of the outer cleat faces and edges since those would have been the areas in constant contact and would rust up fresh after sitting for a while. Overall, the process is really straightforward and most enjoyable. The best part is the results are outstanding and do not take an enormous amount of time to accomplish.

The different rust tones are a result of adding a rust wash to the tracks that have already been treated with *Blacken-it*, it is this interaction that create the textural results.

The tracks are mounted for the final time, the unique appearance further reinforcing the notion this tank was out of commission and languished in the shop.

some final thoughts on the model: ●

• at this point, I've come to the end of a rather long and winding road regarding this project. Many of you probably have similar shelf-queens hanging about, and with the advent of newer injected-molded versions always ready to debut, it is a good idea to keep pace and finish some of these older subjects. The is still plenty of rewards left within them!

• one aspect I focused on with the pigments was to recreate the dirt elements with a hard-edged look to them. Typically this will happen when the dirt is flung up on the vehicle, it stays there, and then moisture (likely rain) will erode the thinner edge layers leaving the denser center section of the dirt. I saw this a lot in the reference photos of Russian tank yards, so I worked hard to replicate this effect by not using a soft cloud effect I would normally do. Applying the pigments dry, then carefully setting them in place with a fixer worked out the best for my goals here. I also tried to keep the areas I added the pigments rather random, like they resulted from falling debris or buildings, common in heavy urban fighting seen during the Chechen wars.

189

oration parts. I prefer to work a small section as much as possible before moving along. I do this because when I used to cover the entire model with just a single discoloration step I found myself going back and forth over the entire model, and I never got the overall sense of what the model would end up looking like. So by switching ideas to finalizing each section at a time as I went along, I became more efficient and could maintain a controlled and balanced level of layered effects over the entire model. Plus, if I stopped each night I had created a reference point for the next sessions, and this would prove invaluable to help reduce the stress levels associated with weathering over time. I simply followed along with the previous section's efforts through to completion, a much easier task in the end.

PIGMENT APPLICATIONS
With the core of the OPR work completed, the upper hull and turret are almost finished I could now turn my attention to the pigments and bringing the lower hull up to par. One of the side benefits of OPR is that the color palette is basically set in place, so it helps us to choose our pigments, and then add in any additional contrasting colors depending on the model's goals. I had some great reference photos of old dried mud stuck in the wheels and tracks of these ex-combat T-72's and that was the look I was going for. To do that requires some extra effort with the pigments to achieve the correct finish, somewhat like the pigments seen on the dozer blade on the D9. It's not overly difficult, and to do this simply means to have the right ratio of pigments on the surface and the correct amount

of thinner/fixer added. Usually, it's my preference to switch to the more dedicated fixers for the task as their adhesion qualities are slightly better than *Tamiya X-20A* thinner, even though my first pigment layer is set with the thinner first. I then build the pigments up on top of this first layer, and for the impacted/cracked/dried look I use more fixer in a wetter application. It should look wet, and not just damp, then after it has set up for about 5 minutes, I very slowly (and from a distance) use the hair dryer on low setting and carefully dry the pigments. This combination of more fixer and faster drying will give them a dried and cracked look.

FINAL DETAILS & TRACKS FITTED

With the end in sight, I treat the tracks in a similar fashion. Because of the prolonged build nature of this project, I had assembled and used *Blacken-it* on the *Friul* tracks years ago, but the process is not required to be done at any real specific moment (basically before you mount them). I would have done the same method if it was current with the painting, and with the tracks at the *Blacken-it* stage, I applied the pigments in the same manner as described above. Lastly, all of the pigments, both on the model and the tracks, are treated with stains and a myriad of flicking to impart a gritty finish to them. It's admittedly one of the more fun tasks to perform. And I love to finalize the last remaining stains, leaking wheel hubs, greasy engine hatches, something about is just fun. Easy to illustrate too!

thoughts on the final elements that bring it all together:

• these are good times, when the end of an involved project comes to the final details, the model becomes a lot more fun, even more than before. I often say it's the last 5% of the work that truly brings out the best in the project and I spend extra time and effort to go around the model and really pick out the ultimate finishing elements, some unseen, but usually it adds just that little bit of *Umph!* It's also the time to make any last second corrections and adjustments, whether in a color tint or stain, or the tracks are not quite fitting right. Each model has some part that almost always needs some further attention. A really good idea, if time permits, is to set the model aside for a few days, and then come back to it and evaluate the finish and see if anything was overlooked or requires a little more love.

193

thoughts on enjoying a long desired subject and fascination with a specific tank: ●

• it's probably fair to say I have a rather broad interest in the different subjects of this hobby. There are some modelers that focus on a very limited array of subjects, or theaters and actions, and for guys like me I have a few favorites strewn amongst the vast array of available kits. The T-72 in its many forms is one that subject for me, I have liked it ever since I read my first *Steve Zaloga* authored books on Soviet-era armor back in the 70's...yes, it's been that long! What's odd is that this is my first completed T-72 based project, but undoubtedly not my last. New T-72/90 kits are arriving as I write this, and it will be hard for me to contain myself, of course, there is always the next Modern Armor title to think about.

T-72B mod.1989   ●

Talk in the streets is that the *Golden Age of Modeling* is fully upon us, we chat and covet each new fantastic release, we stock up on a dizzying array of new painting and weathering products, and in the end we're left to enjoy our hobby to the greatest extent we have ever seen. To further that strength is the united enthusiasms we all share for the joy of building and painting, whether it's an older kit brought up to today's standards, or the latest injected plastic kit of a subject we longed to see, but never really thought it would actually appear in our lifetime. For modern armor builders, this is especially true since the WWII subjects were always a finite category, whereas the modern era continually grows and expands.

Leading the way is *Trumpeter*, and to their credit the last round of modern armor releases beginning with their T-62 & T-64 series make any lover of Post-War Russian armor very happy campers. The T-72 forever embodies the notion of the low-slung big-gunned Russian tanks from the Cold War age, and now as I put the last elements of weathering on my older *Tamiya*-based kit, *Trumpeter* is releasing new-tool kits of this iconic battle tank by the boatload. Golden Era indeed! The T-72 deserves it, the changes it has undergone since it's earliest inceptions (many of which still pop up in the Middle Eastern conflicts), to the latest T-90 versions, it's look is unmistakable and attraction undeniable. So here's to *Trumpeter, MENG, Tamiya, AFV Club*, and the rest of the companies providing us with this true *Golden Age of Modeling*.

RUSSIAN MBT T-72B(mod.1989)

1/35 Tamiya Russian MBT T-72B (mod. 1989)

RUSSIAN T-72B (mod.1989)

CONSTRUCTION

SURFACE PRIMER

CHIPPING FLUID LAYER #1

RED PRIMER

CHIPPING RED PRIMER

CHIPPING FLUID LAYER #2

RUSSIAN GREEN BASE CAMO

GREEN CAMO HIGHLIGHTS

THINNER PAINT WEAR

FINAL CHIPPING

FABRIC AREAS PAINTED

MARKINGS APPLIED

13 RUBBER FENDER PAINTED

14 RUST WEATHERING APPLIED

15 FADED GREEN PANELS

16 RUST CHIPPING APPLIED

17 TURRET RUST APPLIED

18 OPR PALETTE

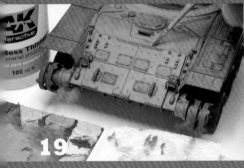

19 OPR PAINT FADING

20 FLICKING PAINT STAINS

21 PIGMENT APPLICATION

22 TRACKS WEATHERED

23 TRACKS FINISHED

24 FINAL MODEL DETAILS

RUSSIAN APC MT-LB(Iraqi)

1/35 Skif MT-LB, Iraqi Army

Model and text by Andy Taylor

Iraqi MT-LB

MT-LB, Mnogotselevoy Tyagach Lekhko Bronirovannyi [multi purpose light armoured towing vehicle was possibly the most numerous Armored Personnel Carrier (APC) used in the Iraq inventory. With its low ground pressure of any APC it was a favourite especially in the more lush softer ground found throughout the country.

CONSTRUCTION

By today's standards the old *Skif* kit used here is very soft in detail, although the actual hull shape and size is pretty accurate, it's lacking many features. These are covered in the following images of the build, main areas requiring attention were the crew access hatch hinges, radiator slatted cover, exhaust outlet (which is completely missing from the kit!), front fenders, brush guards for the main lights, and all the running gear.. Other features were added such as antenna mount, elongated vision slots, and various resin parts taken from the old Armo resin kit...The parts you see on the model are the best bits. All weld beads were added using Plastruct 0.3 rod...

I opted for a set of *Friulmodel* early-style tracks, (the later type track is available from *Miniarm*). Friul also give you a new set of sprockets, which I used but the kit supplied sprocket is quite good enough. The idlers required some work; again the detail was very soft on these parts. I would hasten to add here that the hardest part of this model was building the brush guards in front of the headlight on top of the fenders. A few attempts to get this right! I did have a small etch fret that came with the Armo kit, but these were no good to capture the correct look of welded round bar.

PAINTING

As with all models I build, I usually like to have in mind of where and how I want the model to look...

Markings, such as unit symbols, call signs and any number plates etc are worthy of noting to add colour and uniqueness to the finished piece. Along with crew kit, stowage etc all work together to add realism.

With this in mind, and gathering images sourced from the internet and private collections I had all the information I needed to portray a newly abandoned vehicle on its hurried escape by its crew. Most Iraqi vehicles were abandoned with the crew turning to civilian clothing and sandals, discarding the military kit, boots etc for fear of capture. I tried to capture that look here, with Tarpaulins and sheets adorning the vehicle adding to the feel of a hasty exit.

After many hours of construction the model has lots of contamination from greasy finger marks, dust and filings etc, which need to be rinsed off. Warm soapy water is the key here, eliminating any chance of peeling primer. Choosing the color was quite difficult, I needed to use Tamiya paints due to the effect I was after using the HS technique, which has been covered excellently in Michael's previous **TANKART** volumes, so I won't go into too much detail here.

Tamiya Deck Tan and *Buff* were both contenders, but was never happy with them...a little too brown for the look I was after. In the end after trying a few different tones on a scrap model, I found that a 50/50 mix of *Tamiya XF-15 Flat Flesh* and *XF-2 Flat White* proved to be an excellent choice.

The base color used was *Lifecolor Dark Olive*, as this airbrushes lovely straight from the bottle requiring no thinning. This was left to dry before coating the whole model in *Tamiya* satin varnish. I did wonder if it would cause too much paint peel when using the hairspray technique but using care to scrub too hard I found it still gave me small scratches and chips I was looking for. A note here, the sand paint used on Iraqi armored vehicles was applied in most cases very thinly resulting in a grayish tone as the green paint grins through. Scrubbing the Tamiya paint with a stiff brush once the hairspray technique had been done helped achieve this effect.

It was time to add the markings at this point, the unit marking of red, white and green of the 4th Mechanized was quite easy just requiring careful masking. A little hairspray was also used under these to create some chipping effects.

The yellow call sign was next, I wasn't happy with the yellows from *Tamiya* so opted for *Vallejo Lemon Yellow*, aware that these tend not to work too well using the HS technique, I knew any scrapes and chips would require painting on. This was done with a fine brush and Vallejo pale sand, the white number 9 [commanders vehicle] was painted free hand with *Humbrol* enamels, white with a little flesh mixed in just to knock the harshness of the white down a touch, using enamels aided any mistakes easier to remove and redo if needed.

The number plates proved quite difficult been so small, first the area was masked and Tamiya White was ap-

Lots of effort was made to improve the front hatches and the fender areas.

Scratchbuilt details add a ton of improvements to this old *Skif* kit.

creating the best model out of the only kit available in plastic:

• as noted in the main body of text, the old *Skif* kit needs a lot of work to obtain a higher level of detail, more up to the standards of kits released today. The yellow resin parts from the inaccurate *Armo* kit I found were the only bits worth using, although the barrel was later changed for a resin replacement from *Tahk*.

• I did have the elderly *Eduard* PE set to hand but actually used none of the parts, opting instead to create parts from plastic sheet, rod and strip. With some good references on hand of which plenty exist on the internet, these were not too difficult to achieve. Some parts such as the exhaust outlet with the 2 flaps (that sits next to the radiator slats), tow rope hawser brackets, and some other small detail parts such as pistol ports were missing from the kit, but with a good set of reference images these again proved not to difficult to construct.

running gear…:

• the wheels and tracks are massively improved with the addition of resin wheels from *Masterclub* which need very little clean up to be fitted, and *Friulmodel* white metal track set fit perfectly around the supplied sprocket. The realistic natural sag of the track is evident here.

The extra detail of the resin road wheels and new *Friul* tracks makes all the difference.

The myriad of scratchbuilt details is very evident in this photo, the *Eduard* PE set was only used as a guide to create new or replacement parts.

Adding the missing details goes a long way to bringing this kit up to date.

tips for creating the abandoned stowage and kit:

• there quite a few different mediums on the market that can be used to create the sheets and tarpaulins, the only 1 available to me at the time was superfine white *Milliput*. This is very easy to use with maybe an hour or so working time, this is sufficient to be able to create the desired folds and creases when applying to the model.

• the method I used was to spread a thin layer of talcum powder on a clean piece of styrene and with a brass tube and start to roll out the mixed *Milliput* to a very thin sheet, turning the rolled *Milliput* every so often and adding more powder as I did so to stop the mixture from sticking to both the tube and the styrene sheet. When happy with the thickness of the *Milliput* (remember this needs to be as thin as possible!) I added some detail to the sheet using a thin steel rule and gently pressing the edge of the rule onto the *Milliput* creating the seam approximately 3 or 4 mm from the outer edge. This was then followed by pressing in the eyelets around the border using a small drill bit in a pinvice. Some other details, such as a light liberated from a *Tamiya* T-55, was used for the searchlight in between the 2 front hatches, a clear lens from *Grief* complemented this area.

thoughts on adding the extra stowage and detail:

• careful manipulation of the *Milliput* sheets is needed to avoid the thin piece of epoxy splitting, the best method I have found is to lift the material with a steel rule onto the model, roughly placing it in its correct position. This is followed by gently creating the folds with two No. 1 brushes dipped in water, the *Milliput* can be moved around and pressed over detail, being careful not to mark the putty with the brushes. The sheet can be folded and creased into a very authentic depiction. This method was used on all the Tarpaulins you see on the model.

• at this point, some extra detail work was done to the hatch interior, such as thinning out of the hatch itself before adding the locking handle and torsion spring assembly. Weld beads added using 0.3 *Plastruct* rod, softened with Liquid poly, the weld texture added using a section of thin hollow brass tube shaped at the end and gently pressed into the softened rod.

• various other detail parts were finalized, such as the brush guards situated at the front of the light units above the front fenders, these were the trickiest parts to build! Trying my best to create two of the same size and shape proved difficult, even though I had made a plastic template of the surround. A few attempts were required to get two I was happy with. A small etch fret of the guard was supplied in the *Armo* resin kit, but the 2-dimensional parts didn't look right. Finally two *Tamiya* fuel cans were placed on the sidewall. These were later lashed to the fuel cap guards with cotton thread, and by brushing some thinned PVA glue that hardens the thread and contracts adding the look of weight to the fuel cans.

MT-LB by ANDY TAYLOR

thoughts on painting the MT-LB, any green will do…:

• in most cases, when using dark green as a base color for Soviet vehicles in conjunction with using the Hairspray technique, it's not essential to use a specific shade of green. These are old vehicles and as such the base colors will be heavily faded and worn. Thus, any suitable shade of relative green approximating a close shade is good enough for our use.

• on this project, I opted for a shade of *Lifecolor* green, which sprayed excellent without the need for further thinning. Here we can see the model is progressing steadily and even some unit brigade markings have been added after masking with *Tamiya* tape along with some detail painting of stowage and front tow hooks etc.

quick ref:

• Green:
LC UA267 Dark Olive

• Sand Camo:
XF-15 Flat Flesh
XF-2 Flat White

plied via the airbrush, followed by a small template I made from clear acetate that was slightly smaller than the previously painted white rectangle. This was carefully attached with *Tamiya* low tack tape enabling the *Tamiya Park Green* to be sprayed on. Again using the *White Humbrol* mixed with a little flesh tone to hand paint the Arabic symbols and the stylized version of the triangular Iraqi armed forces device… This actually went better than I thought and I managed to apply them all in 1 go that I was happy with. Phew, I did imagine that with failing eyesight this was going to take a few attempts.

This left quite a bright and stark model, so onto the weathering…As mentioned by Michael previously, many modelers struggle with the best choice of color to use as a starting point for a filter etc…myself included I have to say. Keep it simple is usually the best option, and the ready made products available now make this much easier. I wanted to add some depth to the light sand color, without it becoming too dark, this first step was very important to still attain the des-

On a multi-media project like this one, primer is a must. *Tamiya's* excellent *Surface Primer* is used here.

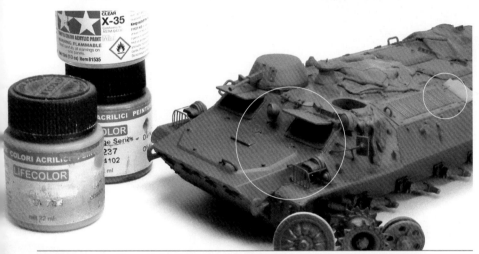

The base green coat is applied, including a satin varnish and then some exhaust rusting as well.

The hairspray layers are applied in two even coats over the entire model, next up is the sand camo paint.

ert look. My choice here was *AK Interactives* streaking grime....although used neat from the bottle used on the test model it left the model far too dark, I opted to try again this time adding 50% thinners, this was the key to the desired effect!. Working it over the entire model moving it around with a larger brush wetted with thinners I started to add streaking effects and feint pin washes around details. Maybe not the correct procedure but seemed to work. This dried quite quickly, so be very precise with the effects you are striving for, some areas I felt were still a little too dark so more thinners was added to the model in effect removing the grime.

Moving onto specific pin washes, again you don't want anything too dark when painting a desert finish, so bearing this in mind I opted for yellow ochre oil with a tiny amount of burnt sienna added, this was applied to bolt heads, hinge details and any recesses on the model, sometimes going back to areas previously applied to a add more depth.

Some parts of the model I felt needed more work adding chipped and scratched areas revealing the original Soviet Green paint underneath, and owing to its brush painting abilities *Vallejo Reflective Green* was used thinned with a little tap water. A good quality brush is a must here, *Windsor Newton* 000 brush is a worth investment... Working methodically through the model at points of high contact such as around

hatches, handles, doors etc, you soon build up lots of tiny dots and marks that with care can be very convincing.

At this point, I chose to add the red color you see on various parts around the model, these are presumably from a past parade, it all added to break up the sand tone and adds another splash of color.

STOWAGE

At this stage, I decided to paint the tarpaulins and sheets that I had made and previously added using *Milliput Super-Fine White* 2-part epoxy putty. These were picked out by hand using *Vallejo Model Color* paints; the green stripes on the blanket/sheet hanging out of the back door was inspired from a few good reference photographs I have showing this pattern to be quite common. Applying the stripes was quite the task, trying to obtain the same thickness in the stripes, I had to keep going back over the white a few times to straighten things up. Once I was happy with this stage of the detail painting, my attention turned to the method and medium to use for the dust on the model.

The sand camo is sprayed on in thin layers to build up the color, now ready for chipping.

tips for a grayish tinge:

• almost all armored vehicles delivered to Iraq were in the standard Russian green, this was oversprayed with a very thin coat of sand color (this shade seems to be very inconsistent). It is the green base color grinning through that gives the vehicles the gray tint to the paint. In fact the motion of scrubbing away at the sand color during the removal using the hairspray technique only added to this effect. Thankfully some excellent choice of colors are available from *Lifecolor* and *Vallejo* that ease the handpainting of detail parts. Two colors from *Vallejo's Panzer Aces* range, *Afrika Korps Green* and a *Khaki* color have been used here on the tarps.

tips on the blackening tracks, easy does it:

• far easier than trying to spray the metal tracks is using this new product from the *AK Interactive* catalog called *Metal Burnishing*.

• simply wash the tracks in acetone first to remove any residual mold release agent, then place them as shown here in the blackening solution thinned 50% with water, although I did find myself adding more of the liquid. The result was superb, not only did it etch the metal a dark metal color, it also added quite a few different hues to the tracks... after which I did a finishing rinse under the tap, and they are now ready for final weathering with some thinned *Humbrol* and pigments to dust them up slightly.

The assembled *Friulmodel* tracks are cleaned of all mold release prior to soaking in the blackening solution.

The various oils and enamels were used to tone, fade and filter the many colors on the painted model.

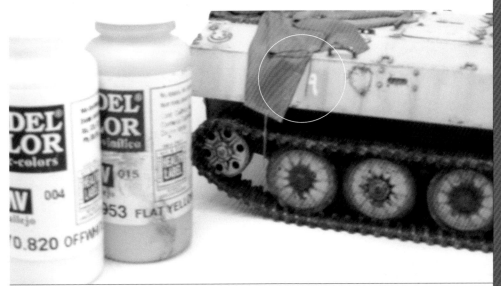

Handpainting the number is accomplished using *Vallejo Model Color* paints and a fine tipped brush.

tips for applying toning, streaks, and filters:

• at this stage, the model starts to achieve some depth and shadows which are an essential path to help create a scale model fool the eye. The added pinwashes around details and layered streaks all combine to slowly build up desired effects.

• *Humbrol 121* was used heavily thinned with enamel thinners to create dust streaks down the sides, this was also built up in various opacities on different parts of the vehicle.

• the white Command vehicle ID number was handpainted after first masking the area and airbrushing the yellow patch. *Vallejo's* don't respond well to the hairspray technique so some subtle chips were painted on after using some of the base color.

thoughts on adding markings:

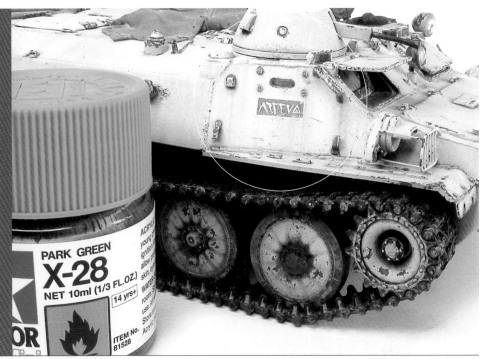

• Many of us will have had a dilemma with decals at some point, sometimes it's not always possible to avoid their use, sometimes the markings are just not available and as a result the only option is to handpaint the various markings yourself. The one marking that was invariably seen on most Iraqi AFV's was the registration plate. This was a green rectangle with white border and generally 3 to 7 arabic numbers (no letters were used), and often carrying the stylized version of the Iraqi armed forces device. I chose to use *Tamiya X-28* here airbrushed on after masking to enable the hairspray technique to chip the paint (this method was used wherever possible). The numerals were then handpainted using *Humbrol* white mixed with a little flesh to take the harshness out of the white. It is far easier to remove the *Humbrol* and start again if any mistakes were made as I painted the numbers, which happened more than once!

The registration plate is handpainted with *Tamiya* and *Humbrol* paints to replicate the worn finish to it.

The base color of the model's sand camo is a blend of *Tamiya XF-15 Flat Flesh* and *XF-2 Flat White*, then lightened and more fading added.

To effectively illustrate the look of an abandoned Iraqi vehicle, some commonly seen items like this blanket in the green stripes was carefully handpainted.

Every area and added detail and stowage must be attended to in order to maximize the results of the construction efforts, yet maintain the visual balance overall.

thoughts on the various procedures coming together to form the completed model:

• the common pattern sheet found on many Iraqi AFV`s has had the green stripes added here, being careful to try and keep the lines similar in width, *Vallejo Reflective Green* was used for this again due to the excellent handpainting qualities of this paint.

• the subtle streaks created earlier in the process are evident here, along with a rear view of the Reg plate. Some darker pinwashes have been applied to add a little more depth to the details on the rear doors, also at this stage the armored glass was made and added to the slots in the rear door and side armor, these were made from clear acetate and attached with PVA glue, and a little dusting was all that was required. The ropes were added to the tarpaulins using the method described earlier to attach the fuel cans.

• the adding of the discarded tarps, accessories and bedding adds a lot to the realism of the model.

215

I have never liked working with powders, or pastel chalks... I find them a bit too hard to control and never sure of the appearance once dry.

A method that has always proven to work for me is *Humbrol* enamels thinned heavily with a good quality white spirit. This was applied sparingly around various features such as lower hull and onto the tarpaulins. It is easy to move the effect around until you are happy with them, as always building up in thin layers drying between coats with an old hair dryer.

At various intervals I used the various base colors mixed with a flesh tone to add some depth to the folds and creases. In effect dry brushing these areas to highlight them. The fuel cans hanging on the side are by *Tamiya*, I needed to remove the wording on the sides prior to painting. These were done in much the same way as the vehicle but adding satin varnish to the paint.

The empty plastic water container is something I made years ago from *Milliput*, and thought it would be a great addition to this model. Sprayed with *Prussian Blue* from *Vallejo*, and using the same mix of *Humbrol* to add some dust effects.

Lots of images of Iraqi MT-LBs show loads of soot and black residue from the exhaust, obviously a sign of neglect and badly in need of a service. This was achieved by first thinning *Humbrol Matt Black* with around 80% white spirit and using this to drag vertical lines down from the outlet, after allowing to dry, more black was added to darken some areas. This was also used around the flaps, and finally a little gloss was added to impart the look of the vehicle been used very recently.

The rusted exhaust flaps (due to the heat) were painted using the *Lifecolor Rust* set, sponged onto the edges, and a thinned filter of *Rust* wash from *AK Interactive*. A little base color was re-applied if I felt I lost too much color, this could then have thin "pin filters" added again.

summary of thoughts on the final model:

• it was my thinking from the start of building this model that it was a vehicle very recently abandoned by its crew for whatever reason. The subtle rusting around the rims that would be in contact with the guide horns on the tracks would soon have a coating of rust on them even after a few hours overnight they would have this effect, so I kept in mind throughout the weathering stages to keep rust to a minimum, just a logical application to the thin sheet metal areas, especially on the exhaust outlet.

217

The front fender was weathered to illustrate the missing bolts and resulting rusting.

TRACKS & WHEELS

After reading a couple of articles regarding the burnishing fluid I felt it was time to give it a go, the *AK interactive* product, the results were superb! Although I had to leave them in the solution for longer than suggested, agitating them every few minutes. Once dried, they are ready for any further weathering; in this case I used *Humbrol 121 Pale Stone*, as used throughout the model. After applying on both sides of the track and left to dry I followed by gently dry-brushing *Humbrol 62* on to the track faces and edges of the guide horns. Just to add the sense of abandonment. The worn steel areas would soon rust after a damp night with no movement.

Road wheels were painted using the same methods as rest of vehicle; the steel rim that comes into contact with the guide horns was then painted using *Mr. Color Steel*, which was polished. Rust would very quickly appear here after a short time in the elements, so *Lifecolor*

thoughts on the final touches of realism:

• Most Iraqi tanks and APC`s show lots of wear and tear, and severe damage to fenders is not uncommon. Due to lack of maintenance exhaust staining especially on flat sided vehicles such as the MT-LB was usually extreme. This was achieved using Humbrol matt black applied in very thin layers allowing the previous coats to dry thoroughly. Lastly, some heavier stains were added with some gloss mixed in to create newer areas of staining, maybe the crew tried a last ditch attempt to start the tired engine to no avail but on doing so created some coughing and spluttering resulting in the emission of oil. Some stronger areas of rust were applied on the bolt holes where the front flap is missing from the fender. I used a very small sponge with tweezers, which is ideal for pinpointing small scratches and rust tones.

Iraqi MT-LB ●

TRACKS & WHEELS cont.

Rust was sponged on randomly before a filter of light rust was applied. The tire's were hand painted using *Vallejo Dark Rubber* before applying dust filters using the same mix as for the tracks..

A feature seen on most Iraqi AFV`s is the dark brown staining around the wheel centres, this is oil/grease from blown seals mixing with dust/sand/dirt. To replicate this I simply airbrushed *Humbrol 98* onto the wheels and carefully wiped excess away with a cotton bud soaked in thinners. A pin wash of *Humbrol Satin Black* around the cap finished off the running gear.

FINAL DETAILS

To finish things off, the fuel cans were lashed using thin cotton and painted to represent nylon cord/rope, and a very thin filter of the sand color to tone it down slightly.

Also at this stage, I felt adding some tie down cords to the tarpaulins would add yet another point of interest. The running gear was added to the model completing what was a very frustrating model to build at times, due to the amount of detail needed to bring out the best of this kit. Hopefully the MT-LB will be visited by *Trumpeter* in the near future...

RUSSIAN APC MT-LB(Iraqi)
Model and text by Andy Taylor

RUSSIAN APC MT-LB(Iraqi)

1 SCRATCHBUILT DETAILS

2 DETAILING INSIDE HATCHES

3 HINGE DETAILS ADDED

4 TARPS & EXHAUST ADDED

5 LIGHTS, GUARDS & WELD BEADS

6 FINAL ASSEMBLY COMPLETED

7 PRIMER COAT

8 BASECOAT OF GREEN

9 HS LAYER #1

10 SAND CAMO APPLIED

11 CHIPPING & PAINTED STOWAGE

12 MARKINGS APPLIED

13

TRACKS ASSEMBLED

14

TRACK BLACKENING

15

BASE COLORS MIXED 50/50

16

ADDITIONAL MARKINGS

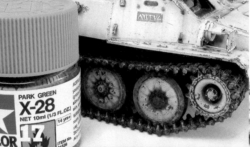

17

REGISTRATION PLATES ADDED

18

FILTERS, DUSTING & FADED PAINT

19

FINAL DETAIL PAINTING

20

DUSTING TARPS

21

FINAL EXHAUST DETAILS

22

ADDITIONAL DUSTING

23

FUEL CANS FINISHED

24

FINAL WEATHERING